T0383841

Achieving Successful Business Outcomes

Achieving Successful Business Outcomes

Driving High Performance & Effective Transformations in a Continuously Evolving Business Environment

Alok K. Sinha

Routledge
Taylor & Francis Group

A PRODUCTIVITY PRESS BOOK

First published 2020
by Routledge
52 Vanderbilt Avenue, New York, NY 10017

and by Routledge
2 Park Square, Milton Park, Abingdon, Oxon, OX14 4RN

Routledge is an imprint of the Taylor & Francis Group, an informa business

© 2020 Alok K. Sinha

Library of Congress Cataloging-in-Publication Data
Names: Sinha, Alok K., author.
Title: Achieving successful business outcomes : driving high performance & effective transformations in a continuously evolving business environment / Alok K. Sinha.
Description: New York, NY : Routledge, Taylor & Francis Group, 2020. | Includes bibliographical references and index.
Identifiers: LCCN 2019052633 (print) | LCCN 2019052634 (ebook) | ISBN 9780367443269 (hardback) | ISBN 9781003009399 (ebook)
Subjects: LCSH: Success in business. | Organizational change.
Classification: LCC HF5386 .S575 2020 (print) | LCC HF5386 (ebook) | DDC 658.4/06–dc23
LC record available at https://lccn.loc.gov/2019052633
LC ebook record available at https://lccn.loc.gov/2019052634

ISBN: 978-0-367-44326-9 (hbk)
ISBN: 978-1-003-00939-9 (ebk)

Typeset in Garamond
by Wearset Ltd, Boldon, Tyne and Wear

"Alok K. Sinha is a name to remember, and *Achieving Successful Business Outcomes* is a tour-de-force. The book is Sinha's impressive intellectual take on essential corporate strategies for the 21st century. Distilled from decades of Sinha's pragmatic business experience, reinventing enterprise after enterprise, this book is not for the faint-hearted. It's the missing manual for CXOs who want to understand the reasons their growth strategies are faltering and how to reinvigorate them."

Steven Sonsino, London Business School, author of *Leadership Unplugged* and *The Seven Failings of Really Useless Leaders*

"Alok has hit the nail on the head! The future demands an entirely new approach to strategic thinking – and MUST be multi-dimensional, multi-faceted and exponential! This does not mean it is devoid of structure. Quite the opposite: in fact, he offers us a comprehensive, relevant and structured way to synthesize the complex forces shaping our future world. It is crucial for leaders to comprehend the interdependencies between a wide range of forces that impact on our future choices and options. More importantly, how these can be used to create optionality and market differentiation. This is a valuable and important contribution to our future relevance toolkit!"

Anton Musgrave, Futurist and Senior Partner, Future World International

"A timely and compelling book that demystifies what it takes to drive change in a volatile and turbulent business environment. Sinha draws on his rich experience and uses simple and effective tools that can be used by anyone looking for a clear and workable business strategy framework to transform your business."

Sudhanshu Palsule, author of *Rehumanizing Leadership*, *The Social Leader* and *Managing in Four Worlds*

"*Achieving Successful Business Outcomes* by Alok K. Sinha offers a well-structured step-by-step guide to help both current and aspiring senior managers develop high performance cultures and transform their organizations to face the challenges and opportunities offered by the continuously evolving global business environment. It is not just a compendium of practical business lessons but also offers a powerful extendable model that can be used to evolve, evaluate and execute risk-calibrated business strategies. Interestingly, it also helps understand why some strategies fail and how to avoid or handle such failures!"

Prof. Piyush Sharma, School of Marketing, Faculty of Business and Law, Curtin University, Australia; Associate Editor (Marketing) – *Journal of Business Research*; Regional Editor – *Journal of Knowledge Management*

"Drawing on his extensive corporate experience, Alok Sinha has written a must-read book for managers. Alok clearly outlines the challenges organizations face in achieving successful business outcomes and what can be done to deal with these challenges. The book develops the key concepts of time, space and action and how these concepts can be integrated to improve performance. The framework and ideas advanced are very innovative, thought-provoking, and relevant in today's highly competitive business environments. This is an important and valuable contribution to improving managerial and organizational effectiveness."

Vinod Singhal, Charles W. Brady Chair, Scheller College of Business, Georgia Institute of Technology

Dedicated to

My pillars of support and inspiration –
Ma, Papa, Babita and Aryan.

Contents

Preface

This book is about achieving *successful* business *outcomes*.

Success and failure are opposite sides of the same coin
– success, a welcome companion; failure, a feared teacher.
Failures and losses, though difficult passages, are as integral
to businesses as are the winning ones, for failures repeatedly
test for perseverance, acumen and change in response.
Success, on the other hand, is based on fundamentally core
organizational ingredients. Thus, whether it is the study
of history or dissection of business cases, the objective is
to analyze the common threads that catalyzed success or
precipitated failure. *However, there is much more to success
than just establishing patterns.*

To begin with, both success and failure are relative.
Achieving the same result may be considered successful by
one and not-so-successful by another based on the individual
criteria of judgement. Hence relying on outcomes, which is
more scientific and accurately definable, is more pragmatic,
robust and without relative bias in measuring the degree of
success.

This book itself is an 'outcome' of the past eight years of
research and validation, although I have drawn its strength
from my rich experience of nearly 35 years and engagement
with organizations and leaders from over 50 countries. My
own lessons on life and business are the result of tutelage
under some very profound teachers only serendipity could

have engineered. From my father for critical essentials to live life, to a Rinpoche for critical knowledge to understand life, to some of the greatest leaders of global standing for critical levers to touch lives. I had the opportunity to interact with hundreds of customers, leaders, practitioners, strategists, thinkers and academicians at close quarters and have tried to learn why some of them were highly successful while others not as much. One common denominator among all was a few simple rules each one had developed that helped them navigate through the complexity of their businesses or in simplifying their lives. Yet another was a keen sense in distinguishing between the rhythm of the natural and the unnatural.

Organizations have traditionally relied upon basing their objectives on a well laid out strategy, the inputs to which are the organizational SWOT (strength, weakness, opportunities and threats). Few organizations achieve all their objectives in entirety, fewer still achieve it on a sustained basis over larger tracts of time, and organizations rarely continue to do the same thing without significant changes to their core assumptions and lifelong operating models. There are many reasons for this.

Researchers have paid special attention to classifying specific 'periods' when studying themes. Simply defined, a period is a length of intervening time span during which specific occurrences or people and advances in various facets of arts, sciences, commerce or finance, etc., are researched or documented. It is not only important to study the period and the transitions therein but also the causes of transition from one period to the next and the rate of those transitions; the former indicates the catalyst for change or innovation causing the transition, while the latter provides a critical pointer as to how quickly maturity was achieved from the state of infancy. The shorter the transitions, the closer the hypothesis or the research was to its ultimate maturity. *A series of short transitions succeeded by a longer one signifies a breakthrough in research followed by a period of sustained use*. Hence it is not only important to study using contemporary time frames, but also the ones before and after the period under study to review the rate of transition. This method is frequently used as a marker over the course of this book to chart progression and identify impending changes in the business environment and is referred to as *competition-changer*.

The other reason why studying occurrences in a contemporary time frame gives fallacious results is due to period bias, defined as *time think*. It was not just a casual occurrence that contemporary thinkers, writers, scientists and painters of the same era found themselves locked with common themes; these scholars were guided by most pressing needs of the society of those times. Thus, what was important for the period may or may not have been the topmost concern in the preceding or the succeeding periods. Sometimes emboldened by a breakthrough in research, the needs mutated from one form into another; however, this can become clearly visible only when the occurrences are viewed across a large tract of time with many intervening periods. Take, for example, medical research over the past two centuries – it began purely as research on diseases (mostly by biologists and doctors), which was transformed into medical devices (like X-ray machines and MRI devices) for minimally intrusive or non-intrusive methods of detecting diseases and abnormalities (primarily engineering led), thus transitioning from doctor-led diagnostics to machine-aided diagnostics. Many periods later saw the focus shifting to inhibiting diseases by the study and manipulation of genes via genetic re-engineering, which has now metamorphosed into wellness and increased longevity through retardation of natural cellular death and other mechanisms.

The critical question here is, which historical markers need to be tracked when studying across periods that have the potential to further transform in the future? I categorize this as *generative transformations*, something that has the innate momentum to push the boundaries of scientific advancements and has the power to benefit all. This is in absolute contrast to *disruptive transformations* which are like impulse changes that break down the current order.

As periods transitioned from one to the next, they were generally marked with a progressively better quality of life and thinking. Wisdom grew at an exponential rate and so did its applications. People learned from each other. *But it was the rapid propagation and adoption that was accelerating progress.* Alex Pentland, an expert on Social Physics, calls this the "wisdom effect," or social learning, where copying people who are successful can yield success faster. He shows, the wider and more diverse the network is to learn from, the higher the chances to outperform.

However, *what was deemed to be a competitive advantage within a specific period ceased to be so in the subsequent ones.* Hence new research and insights were continuously needed for any civilization to stay progressive and ahead. This approach continues to be extremely important even today, though with finer techniques, for evaluating investments into research, new products or starting up an organization. A new evolving trend, *attitudinal economics*, is quietly disrupting some of the core doctrines, where new producers have no hesitation in giving away what seems to be their competitive advantage or are attacking the traditional industries by breaking down every assumption linked to their supposedly long-term competitive advantage. One such example is the community-enabled open-source and pay-what-you-want formats (e.g., Netflix willingly giving away their design of micro-services or Chaos Monkey to the programming community). Another example is Elon Musk with his outrageous thinking in enabling future energy to be delivered nearly free via cheap and long-lasting solar cells and hence disrupt the power giants of today.

There are two ways to execute research – both equally favored. The first one, entails identifying successful companies and studying them over multiple parameters to find common levers of success across them. However, this can have a finite shelf life as over time environments change and models break down due to *time think*. There are many examples of successful companies in a specific decade that lost steam in the subsequent one and some that even evaporated. The second method for research is selecting pertinent parameters from existing models in allied fields – hence inherently stable – and combined for its applicability to the field under research. The model is first verified for data in the past followed by testing it for data in the current and correlating with outputs in the future. I adopted the latter, and the *STA strategy triangle* or the *space–time–action model*, has been tested in real time over the past eight years. Thus, the book will obviously be relevant for a longer period.

The STA model possesses the inherent capability of representing reality and capturing change – critical in managing fast-changing environments; and the core of the model is to help navigate effectively through such rapidly changing business environments. Unlike traditional business studies that use a single lens to define business rules or organizational practices, it uses the combination of *space, time and action* – and hence abbreviated *STA*, as the driver of outcomes – something fundamental and core to human thinking across the ages (Albert Einstein, Herbert Spencer, Aristotle, Henri Lefebvre or even in the game of chess). I have modified it for its applicability to business. This combination of the fundamental dimensions of space, time and action provides for a powerful business strategy framework, where space represents a firm's operational territory and hence strengths, time represents market state and operating conditions, hence opportunities, and action represents execution thus mimicking lifecycle. The model is a natural model and hence fits beyond the dictates of business too.

Within the space, time and action, lies the nuanced art of judgment and decision-making, both in stable and volatile environments. This involves choices, trade-offs and planning across multiple horizons and consequently answering the key questions of business interests – growth, scale and scaling. Space, time and action are not standalone tools, the combination of *time–space, space–action, time–action* and *time–space–action*, gives rise to highly incisive and unique views to calibrate strategy and execution. When taken three-at-a-time there are 27 potential strategies possible. Depending upon the environment, objectives and the prevailing market conditions, the likely choices can be narrowed down to a few. This is where *elastic strategy* comes in as the final choice reflects the leader's makeup and risk-outcome bias.

While the book can easily be an inflight read, the intention is for it to be a constant companion in the day-to-day running of the business theater; whether the times are in recession, or stable or in expansion, or, the strategy being devised is for own or adjacent or truly unknown spaces; whether the environment is stable or volatile, or whether it is the strategy, its operationalization, or its execution; whether it is continual improvement, re-engineering or innovation that is the desperately needed rightful action or whether it is generative or disruptive transformation that needs to be adopted, both the applicability and the choices are covered. It is also important not to be sucked into traps knowingly or inadvertently – one doesn't know what one doesn't, but it is important to continuously scan to avoid blind spots.

The future will be different. Many of today's jobs will cease to exist. The scope of community and the community interactions will change. And large-scale convergence and substitution will become pervasive. This book has both theoretical and practical applications, the former that can help propel further research and analysis, while the latter can help practicing leaders drive their firms forward confidently in any environmental conditions. It will also help casual readers understand how the future is evolving and how different organizations are responding to this change.

Readers that would benefit from this book:

- Top and senior leaders in established organizations
- Start-up CXOs
- Management students
- Aspiring leaders
- Leadership coaches
- Casual readers interested in understanding what the future holds and the new ways of responding to it.

Acknowledgments

I wish to express my sincere gratitude to Shreyas Gandhi, Bangalore, Professor Steven Sonsino of the London Business School, Professor Ashish Sinha of University of Technology, Sydney, and Chandra Sekhar Ramachandrani, New Delhi, for their review and valuable suggestions.

Thanks to Mr. Ratan Tata, Chairman Emeritus, Tata Sons, for allowing me to quote an internal business planning meeting – to exemplify a 'what they don't teach you at business schools' moment; Professor Tasos Kokkalis, Head Flight Science and Simulations, University of Glasgow, for lengthy insights on 'what an aircraft stall is' and lessons on 'how to make an aircraft stable' through his legendary use of simple paper airplanes and chewing gum – plain brilliance! To Lalit Jalan, advisor and former CEO, Reliance Infrastructure, for helping me reconstruct a behind the scenes – 'how to erect and operationalize a refinery in half the time?' example.

Thanks to Amit Kumar, an expert researcher in advanced autonomous cars, for his deeply thought-provoking discussions on 'who are we to decide (or algorithmize) if an autonomous vehicle should kill a life to save its occupant?'

Special thanks to my acquiring editor at Taylor & Francis, Kristine Mednansky, and her team across Chicago, New York, Boca Raton and the UK, including Katherine Kadian and Carly Cassano, as well as Pip Clubbs of Wearset and my copy editor, Ting Baker, for their valuable suggestions and guidance during the production of this book.

Lastly, with utmost gratitude, I am deeply indebted to my father, Dr. J.K. Sinha, and my wife, Babita, for their immense patience in repeatedly reading the manuscript through its countless revisions and innumerable changes and recommending copious edits.

There are many others too and I thank all of them for their time and suggestions.

About the Author

Alok K. Sinha has held multiple CXO positions in global companies in the immediate past, including Chairman and CEO of a listed software company with entities around the globe. He has worked with large and prestigious global companies. A hands-on leader in the Technology and Software industry with a nearly 35-year track record in driving successful outcomes in the areas of leadership, business management and strategy, he has profitably ramped and managed many end-to-end businesses, from seeding enterprises, turning around and growing organizations, managing global sales, engineering and delivery teams, in the Manufacturing (Automotive and Aerospace), Software Product Engineering, Logistics, BFSI, Government, Foods and Beverages, and Education domains. He is as an active investor and advisor to several start-ups.

Sinha has been credited with creating a highly successful innovation program in his previous companies, which generated multiple thousands of man-days of cutting-edge innovation outputs and patents every year. He instituted a unique 'reverse' mentoring program for his top management by the millennial workforce. Sinha has also been actively engaged in teaching and devising management development programs. He formulated and implemented a very successful mini-CEO program that has helped turnaround sinking, negative EBIT firms into high-growth and highly profitable organizations. He has contributed to articles in local and global media with perspectives on life, management, leadership and areas of growth like Organizational Blueprinting and Strategy, Engineering Services, IoT and Education. He is also a visiting professor at various business schools.

Sinha is an Electrical Engineering graduate from Punjab Engineering College, Chandigarh, and a postgraduate in Business Management from XLRI, Jamshedpur, India.

IN SEARCH OF SUCCESSFUL OUTCOMES

"Vision is not enough, it must be combined with venture. It is not enough to stare up the steps, we must step up the stairs."

– *Václav Havel*

Chapter 1

The Never-Ending Cycle of Creation, Sustenance, Destruction and Transformation

1.1 Navigating through the Haze of Chaos

The Airbus 330 Air France plane had just entered a turbulent zone, as cautioned earlier by the commanding pilot minutes before he had left for the rest cabin to get his scheduled break. For the other two pilots this weather condition was nothing new, but as they geared for an adequate response, something unexpected happened. The aircraft's autopilot suddenly disengaged and so did the auto-thrust system within the next few seconds. Little did the pilots realize, due to formation of ice in the pitot tubes (these tubes measure airspeeds), the sensors were giving incorrect readings and the on-board computers were erroneously sensing lower speeds, triggering the auto-pilot to disengage. Following his natural instinct, one of the pilots in a desperate attempt to increase speed and reverse the descent, pushed the throttle stick further, injecting more fuel and driving more power from the aircraft's engines. But the aircraft warning system was continuously screaming an aerodynamic stall.

The 101 of the pilot's manual describes the standard procedure under stall conditions is to nosedive first, gather downwards momentum and then fly back up again. The black boxes retrieved later from the bottom of the Atlantic two years after this incident confirmed no such maneuver had been attempted. In fact, the aircraft hit the ocean exactly 3 minutes and 30 seconds after the first warning signal with its nose up, engines in full throttle, in an aerodynamic stall. The investigators later surmised that the angle at which the aircraft was ascending, or its angle of attack, was so extreme, that the computers were rejecting the data and erroneously stopping the stall warning, *despite* the aircraft being in a stall. Only when the pilots were reducing the angle of attack were the on-board computers recognizing the data as correct and resuming the stall warning. This unfortunate negative feedback did not allow the plane to come out of its stall until the point of impact. Just a minute before the impact, the captain, back in the cockpit, had realized the fatal maneuver that the co-pilot had made.

> 02:13:42 "No, no, no… Don't climb… no, no."
> 02:13:43 "Descend… Give me the controls… Give me the controls!"
> A new hazard warning >>> 'ocean surface approaching'…
> 02:14:23 "Damn it, we're going to crash… This can't be happening!"
> 02:14:25 "But what's going on?"
> 02:14:27 "Ten degrees of pitch…"

This was the last human voice on the black-box recorders. The last command, incomplete, probably in a desperate effort to avoid the ocean. But the flight was doomed. It had already touched the ocean surface. The result – a tragic loss of lives and watery graves for the crew and the 228 passengers on board somewhere at the bottom of the Atlantic.

*

Life and businesses are shockingly similar in many ways. If left unchecked, both could sink through a rapid descent; and if sensors and the reported metrics start giving erroneous readings, the outcome could be pure chaos. This is what had likely occurred in the cockpit of the ill-fated Air France flight, scripting a tragic outcome. Leaders face such demanding situations continuously. Worse still, the effectiveness of their response in such crises, which is critical to mitigate and reverse the chaos, is delivered under extreme duress when both the response quality and its outcomes are known to suffer. The key question unraveled in this book is, how can outcomes be successfully managed in the face of unknown, chaos or even chance occurrences?

Navigating in space is exponentially more difficult than navigating on the road – because there are too many directions to investigate, too many unknowns to be prepared for and infinite pathways to chart in the spatial system. So it is with business. Business environments are extremely demanding and change is continuous, precipitated constantly by an innumerable number of actors and conditions. To be prepared for sharp responses in challenging situations, continuous scanning of the business and the environment, and their impact on the intended *outcome* needs to be closely monitored.

Outcome has been expounded most precisely in statistics. It represents the set of unique results that are possible in a probability experiment. When a die is cast, it can have six possible outcomes. When it is thrown repeatedly and the results tabulated for the number of times each face occurred, the resulting graph is a frequency distribution graph. Abraham de Moivre, the eighteenth-century statistician, noticed that the probability of such events traced a distribution curve that resembled a bell-shaped graph – a very important mathematical discovery (Figure 1.1). This behavior, also termed the normal distribution curve, states that within a statistically relevant sample, 50% of the population will lie to the left of the sample-mean and the other 50% to the right of the mean. If one were to pick up a random sample of a hundred leaves or a similar number of birds – in fact, anything, stones, people, students, etc., for any measure of their performance criteria – marks, quality, size, color, etc., 50% of the sample would be below average and 50% above the average of the sample. Furthermore, the 10% on the extreme left of the distribution graph depicts the bottom measure, and the 10% at the extreme right of the graph denotes the top measure, while the rest are distributed uniformly between the two, around the mean. Its application in business has an equally profound significance: given any 100 companies, ten will be wiped out, ten will excel and the remaining 80 will survive between 'just about' to 'reasonably

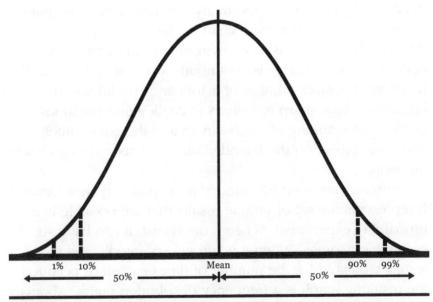

Figure 1.1   The Ubiquitous, Normal Distribution or the Bell Curve

well enough.' Thus, just a few firms are destined to survive, coded by nature itself. The search then is, how can a firm improve its chances of success and find a spot for itself in the extreme right corner of the normal distribution curve?

Outcomes are the result of both the choice of an *action* and the action itself (occasionally, inaction too). There are only three atomic actions possible – creation, sustenance and destruction (more conventionally, initiation, persistence and conclusion). These three actions are not only starkly different in their outcomes, but also need very different *inputs* to instantiate and propel them.

Creation signifies novelty, acumen and innovation. It demands knowledge, research or intellect to create something new. Studies of successful start-up businesses have highlighted a few core ingredients within their composition – a well-designed product needed by the market, knowledgeable founders and core employees, a structure that scaled well with their scaling growth and a disciplined approach to spend. All rely upon knowledge and understanding – pedagogical, mentored and experiential, embodied within the team. Big money comes in the subsequent step, literally.

Sustenance signifies nourishment and growth. Sustenance needs essential resources to be regularly secured and replenished, like food. In the jungle an animal needs to hunt and eat to stay alive, a human being needs to work to earn wages and keep the family provided for, while a business needs to produce and sell goods and services to make profits and keep it running. Thus, sustenance signifies the need for tangible resources or money supporting life as well as the growth of the start-ups or any business-as-usual running of an organization.

Destruction, closure or death may seemingly need nothing. But it does; it needs courage, strength and sometimes fearlessness, particularly if voluntarily initiated. Death signifies detachment, which is a difficult art. Death does not necessarily mean demise only of the mortal body or a business entity but could be of a culture steeped in lethargy, a product being retrenched at its end-of-life, of penury and suffering, or just, a change in the mindset. It could even mean retiring products well before the market gets tired of them, an act that Steve Jobs was very adept at.

These three atomic actions have universal applications. They represent the repetitive lifecycle of all beings. Every lifecycle begins at birth and ends at death; in-between the two states, an entity sustains itself through growth and expansion. Business software applications, for example, use the same three atomic transactions – addition, amendment (or manipulation) and deletion of records, at their core. Any other action is a derivative, a combination or in support of these three.

However, there is one more action – *enquiry* – that does not directly alter the end-state and hence is not an atomic action but is critical in catalyzing a successful outcome. Enquiry refers to research and/or self-reflection. It is followed by data-sensing and data-capture. Then comes the inference (or sense-making) and subsequent reporting that drives calibrated actions. When the enquiry is based on incorrect assumptions and the data reported incorrect, the inference and the consequent outcome will too be incorrect. This is also what happened to the ill-fated Airbus 330.

The atomic actions can be combined to form more complex actions. Change is the law of nature and signifies evolution. Whenever change is significant, with the new entity being very different from the original in its structure or characteristics (e.g., a larva turning into a butterfly, or closer to our topic, Apple becoming a music distribution company instead of a company that sells computing devices), such changes are termed as transformations. *Transformation* thus can be defined as a termination or end-of-life followed by rebirth or reinvention. Transformation is an extremely critical lever for step progression and is a vital complex action.

***Action**, hence, is the first of the three core dimensions in managing successful outcomes.*

All beings need a habitat to live and grow in, including business organizations. They need to undergo regular evolution and transformations for them to survive. The answer lies in the *space* they operate in. For businesses, space represents the interplay of three domains – the markets where firms operate in, the mind of the consumer where his 'needs' and 'wants' exist, and the environment that comprises competitive and regulatory compulsions. The contours of space are continuously changing due to the evolving needs of the customers, the intensely competitive actions and the changing regulatory compliances, and firms need to continuously respond to these changes. Space needs to be continuously monitored, protected and over time expanded. *Managing **space** is the second core dimension of delivering successful business outcomes.*

A final deliberation on action – which phase does a successful business spend most of its time in? A life is deemed successful if it has lived its full share and achieved broadly whatever it had set out to. Compared to the process of birth and death, the maximum amount of time is spent in nourishing and sustaining it, which includes nurturing, growth, maturing and reinventing (or transforming) through the passage of chaos. Since the sustenance or the preservation phase is the longest in any lifecycle, it is the also the most difficult and uncertain phase. Organizations are bombarded by a continuous stream of change and uncertainty, both internal and external, which needs to be effectively responded to. This forms a key metric for a well-run and successful sustenance. It is also impossible to preserve anything in permanence because time itself is the biggest destroyer. An iron nail gets rusted over time, a person ages, liquids evaporate and disappear, and unused grains gets decayed; so too do machines, operations and firms. To keep something running well and preserved even in its current state, needs a lot of sustenance effort.

With time being a perpetual catalyst for degradation, firms often find themselves missing the beat on markets, people, costs, expansion opportunities and other business areas. They resort to making large-scale changes to their internal as well as external strategies. The traditional firms call it transformation while the start-ups call it as pivot. Old thinking, inefficient processes and irrelevant structures are terminated and replaced by the new. Multiple researchers have confirmed that firms in general have rarely survived across multiple periods; only the ones that have reinvented or transformed themselves regularly, do. *Time, thus, encapsulates value that needs to be extracted continuously and is the third core dimension in managing business outcomes.*

Action, space and time have thus a definitive link to success and outcomes in businesses, in fact, as will be seen, in all walks of life, sciences or humanities; they are hence the fundamental variables that drive outcomes – the essence of this book. The quest is to configure an effective model for managing successful outcomes.

1.2 The Strategy Triangles – Combining the Three Fundamental Variables to Control Outcomes

Space, time and action are the three *fundamental variables* that control outcomes and can effectively model business strategy and help navigate its execution – the core of this book. This simple model can represent a comprehensive mechanism in formulating, devising, and adjusting business strategy and actions in real time.

The combination of space, time and action have been pervasively fundamental to human thinking. They find their earliest documented existence in Aristotle's "three unities" constructed for writing drama –the unity of space, the unity of time and the unity of action. He ruled that a play must restrict itself to space representing one place and not compress geography, must depict actions occurring within a time span not over 24 hours and must have only one plot or action. The underlying emphasis in adopting such a constraint was to apply focus, adopt simplicity and enable the ease of execution.

A very comparable combination – of space, time and *force* (instead of *action*), is central to strategy formulation in the game of chess too. The most obvious element, force, is the superior strength displayed on the chessboard space due to careful management of the chess pieces; it is greatest when all the pieces together display a remarkable teamwork. Space refers to the number of squares on the chessboard controlled by a player's pieces; space and force go hand in hand. Finally, time. Time is critical as the faster a player establishes control over the board, the better are his chances of winning. Thus, the tempo and timing of both are critical.

Far from the realm of board games, and into the core of science and metaphysics, space–time–force have continued to dominate their presence. Einstein's *spacetime* model combined space and time into a single four-dimensional continuum, with three dimensions arising out of space and one from time. The model postulated that an object travelling at the speed of light experiences time at a much slower rate. That meant, time, like space, is a variable. Einstein considered the 'General Theory of Relativity' a big accomplishment for himself because it complied with Newton's 'action–reaction' (AR) theory, which he felt, was earlier violated by his 'Special Theory of Relativity.' Space–time–force (action–reaction) remained central to his postulates. The proof is slightly difficult to conceptualize because visualization in four dimensions is not easy.

Much before Einstein, meta-physicist and philosopher Herbert Spencer viewed the interplay of *time, space, matter, motion and force* as a fundamental block that drove outcomes. Spencer argued that everything in the material world was relative. *Time* abstracts *sequence* and is not reversible. *Space* abstracts *co-existence of matter* and can be traversed in all directions. *Force* is responsible for motion of the matter (*change* in position or state). While Spencer stopped short at this juncture, a simple extension makes this postulate analogous to the current proposition of fundamental variables i.e., *action* abstracts *force* – as force *cannot* exist without action. Thus, the combination of space, time and action like Spencer's and Einstein's time, space and force is capable of driving outcomes.

Four examples above, show four different instances, where the fundamental variables – space, time and action – drive outcomes in humanities, a strategy game, science and metaphysics realms, other than our postulations in business. It essentially possesses the inherent capability of representing reality, capturing change and driving outcomes.

For the ease of representation, the fundamental variables – time, space and action, have been plotted on three axes, 120 degrees apart. This template is referred to as the **'space–time–action strategy triangles'** depicted in Figure 1.2. Each axis is represented by a triad of three states that covers completely, end-to-end, the entire gamut of possible occurrences, from one extreme to the other. The strategy triangles will also be referred to as the STA strategy triangles or simply STA triangles in the text.

The space, time and action axes together also have the power to model beyond just the business context, the core intent of this book. Some of its applications can be evidenced later in the book (e.g., STA triangles for the evolution cycle of the universe) while others like space as personal consciousness are beyond the scope of this book.

The STA strategy triangles model provides for three extremely powerful examination lens, one each for the three fundamental dimensions of space, time and action. This is like

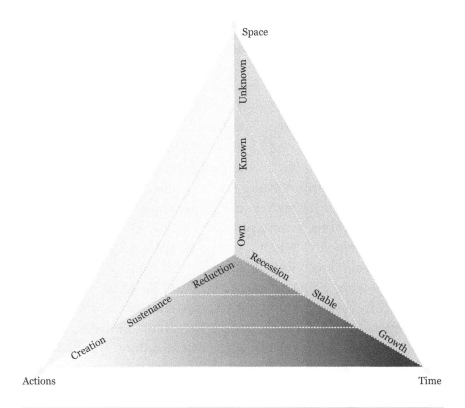

Figure 1.2   The Strategy Triangles

using the regular light, the ultraviolet light and the Infrared light for inspection. An artwork is inspected under UV light to detect alterations or damage, normally invisible under regular light. Similarly, infrared light binoculars, also known as thermal imagers, are used for night viewing. They detect longer wavelength light, normally invisible to our eyes, even from objects in complete darkness, making them visible. The three light sources reveal three different characteristics of the object being viewed.

Likewise, traditional business studies use a specific lens to research and define business rules or organizational phenomena and practices; by a single dimension one means that business management concepts can in general be mapped onto one of the three axes – of time, of space, or of action. By representing an enterprise as an integrated combination of time, space and action(s), the same laws can be applied simultaneously to all three axes, which can now unearth more complete dimension of managing business. As an example, *group think*, is a psychological behavior where a homogenous group ends up taking illogical decisions just to maintain the harmony of the group and where dissent is neither aired nor appreciated; this is a business construct on the action axis. However, the group think theory opens amazing extensions when applied to the time and space axes simultaneously. When a group of organizations within a similar space, are blind-sighted by thinking in a similar fashion they are guilty of *space think* and liable to be disrupted by an external agent (e.g., what Amazon did to booksellers like Borders or Barnes & Noble). Similarly, *time think* gives fallacious results when organizations are guilty of having an anachronous view of the markets despite changing competition and customer needs; this blind-sightedness is caused due to the study of occurrences limited to a time period and Kodak or Sony are distinct examples of being afflicted by such a malady. Such an approach of extending existing unidimensional inferences of a study or a phenomenon into multi-dimensional implications helps in providing significantly finer inputs for immediate, short and long-term business planning. Such simple extensions are liberally dispersed within the book.

The book focusses on how to survive, thrive and drive the market. Not only space, time and action are usable as standalone tools but the combination of time–space, space–action and time–action and finally, time–space–action, gives rise to incisive views. But it is most important to understand these foundational elements first.

An implicit corollary intrinsic to the preceding paragraphs is, since the model converts 'unidimensional business elements or business phenomena' into rich 'three-dimensional business constituents,' the 3D view is always clearer than a unidimensional or 2D view because there are 'minimal hidden planes and views,' something that will be evident to the readers as they go through this text. For example, during the times of recession, should a firm invest in innovation or continue in its path of optimizing costs only? What other options exist for a firm outside of innovation and optimization? How can transformation be used effectively as an option? These are efficiently handled by the model and discussed in ample details.

There is also an effort to create a 'business-model-twin,' something distantly analogous to the 'digital twin.' The digital twin technology is a huge advancement in creating digital replica of a machine (e.g., a pump, or an environment, such as an office space). So far, design and test simulation had been purely static – given the operating and boundary conditions of a machine being built, computer-aided design and simulation helped in optimizing better yet cheaper products. With the advent of Internet of Things (IoT) devices and the capacity to store and crunch large data, the simulation of critical installations in real time is now possible. As the machine (pump in our example) continues to operate in the live environment, important machine parameters are continuously tapped and stored via an IoT interface. Data analytics and AI is then used to predict behavior and run what-if analyses to evaluate a range of probable outcomes. However, as business environments are very complex and dynamic, modelling it in its utmost entirety yet seems to be a few scientists away. The STA triangles may evolve into a full-blown business-twin as it has the power to model and manage business strategy and its execution in real time.

Within the space, time and action dimensions, lie the delicate art of judgment and decision-making, both in stable as well as in volatile environments. Decision-making involves choices and trade-offs. However, it is also a mix of rational as well as spontaneous responses that not only relies upon logical reasoning but is also affected by energy, the environment and emotions.

The next section deals with the nuances of planning across multiple horizons or answering some of the key questions of business interests – growth, scale and scaling. This also deals with balancing market engagement strategies based on the state of the market.

Then comes the mechanism to identify and avoid the dreaded encirclements and entrapments. Encirclement is a war strategy that is used to cordon off enemy from all sides giving it no chance of escape. Encirclement is dangerous – both in encircling the enemy or getting encircled. Since encirclement signifies a certain death, slow or otherwise, the encircled forces have nothing to lose; their actions are desperate and not necessarily calibrated. Hence such situations must be avoided at all costs. Organizations get entrapped and encircled due to overestimation of their strengths and underestimation of the threats; it is also critical to keep close tabs on dysfunctional decision-making and avoid getting blindsided by group think, space think and time think, which is also evaluated in significant detail in the text.

Finally, the spotlight is turned on how an organization needs to stay relevant and reinvented in a continuously evolving business environment and why reinventing and transformation is needed. It is also important to understand the relative differences between, continuous improvement, re-engineering, innovation and transformations – all of which are very different from each other. Transformations can be both generative as well as disruptive. The text especially dives into the details of types, characteristics and the mechanisms of catalyzing such transformations, a view that is quite different from the existing texts. Finally, it is not only the organizations but even human beings who need to continuously transform themselves. It is a life skill.

The last is a culmination of all that is discussed in the book (i.e., the STA strategy triangles in their entirety). Time signifies truth and the state of the market, whether, in recession, stable or growth. However, space and action signify choice. This gives rise to a potential 27 different combinations to choose from; not all are prescriptive. Under recessionary or loss-making conditions, protecting the core is the lowest minimum strategy but something more is needed. The stable market state is all about ecosystem expansion with linear and non-linear amplification. This is also the region where firms spend the bulk of their lifecycle maintaining and expanding their position across multiple time periods. The growth market periods correspond to firms not only playing in its areas of strength and interest, but also in unknown or semi-known spaces. Though this is the cruelest region and many enterprises venturing in this region fail, it is also the region of hope, discovery, innovation and curiosity. In short, it is all about breakout, disruption, aggression, attack and annexation of competition, or an elusive solution, an antidote to a dreaded disease or just a change in attitude. But is staying within the precincts of the strategy triangles enough? Existing research shows that it is not. We use the concept of elasticity to define the *elastic coefficient of strategy*, which is the *distance from the core strategy*, beyond what is considered minimum. The more the elastic coefficient, the greater is the risk and the rewards.

1.3 In Summary

- Running a business well does not necessarily means a plethora of metrics to track. The key is to pick the relevant top few levers; the more difficult part is finding those few.
- Response under crises is delivered under extreme duress when both quality of response and its outcomes are known to suffer.
- Business outcomes are a result of actions (or inactions).

- There are only three atomic actions – creation, sustenance and destruction (or simplification).
- The three atomic actions need three different input resources as their fuel
  - Creation needs knowledge, research and intellect
  - Sustenance needs food and money as well as reinventing oneself continuously.
  - Destruction needs courage, strength and fearlessness.
- Transformation is a complex action, which is akin to destruction followed by rebirth.
- Successful businesses spend the maximum amount of time in sustenance mode, nourishing and reinventing themselves. Managing this continuously is critical for survival.
- Time represents value that needs to be continuously released. Since time is a catalyst for perpetual degradation, sustained sustenance and innovation is a difficult task.
- Space represents markets where firms operate in; space changes due to the evolving needs of the markets as well as regulatory compulsions. Hence firms need to continuously innovate and reinvent themselves.
- Time, space and action have been a fundamental part of human thinking from olden times and have their applicability in theatre, chess, science and meta-physics, and can be easily used as a framework to model business strategy and execution.
- Time, space and action have a strong correlation to successful outcomes and can be represented on the STA strategy triangles to model business.

Chapter 2

Time, Space and Action

Experience, Boundary and Force

It had been a testing week. The business plan for one of the Tata group companies had been presented to the Chairman, Mr. Ratan N Tata, for the third time and this time too he had denied acceptance. His ask, a specific target market share with consequent revenues and a certain profitability goal. The Chairman, a calm but very sharp leader, began to then explain why the target market share and minimum net profitability were key indicators for sustained business preservation and how they cleverly encompassed every element of business planning and execution.

The *market share*, he explained, was a composite representation of year-on-year growth, the state of the industry, the level of difficulty posed by the Chairman himself and the resulting revenues generated out of this – and not just any revenues. It also implied capital expenditure and advance capacity planning, as sales cannot always be uniform and do not necessarily coincide with production capacity, and a horde of other dependent variables including understanding of external factors and short- and long-term market trends.

Profitability is a constraining and contra-balancing variable. Even if an organization had achieved the levels of required profitability in the previous years, salary indexation, rising input costs, investments, etc., would invariably make it impossible to achieve the feat without making changes. The gap would result in production teams wanting higher sales-realization, and sales wanting lowered costs of production. Each position would help spawn threads within their own organizations to operationalize methods in achieving these opposing goals. Production needed to look at cost reduction via value engineering, import substitution, procurement rationalization, supplier negotiations, just-in-time supplies, lower rejections, rework and warranties, etc., while the sales people needed to look at reduced discounts and freebies, efficient debtor collections, more sales reach and increased sales. The two metrics thus were not only the initial seeds to a business plan but also a subsequent trigger for downstream operational and sales plans. It could be possible that the desired profitability was a couple of years away but the sustained plan of *action* to get to those levels were important and something the Chairman wanted to see.

The Chairman finally added that once the plan of action was frozen it may not always be possible to execute without making changes to it downstream during the year. If the economy hit a downturn, he would expect the businesses to maintain the agreed market share percentages, even though the sales volume would be numerically lower. With tough external conditions, protecting profitability would always be a difficult task as businesses cannot proportionately scale down at a flick of a switch, but the adjustments to the plan should try to maintain the profitability with as little degradation as possible. Two core business metrics to manage an enterprise! An elegant and great way to run a conglomerate.

*

Most seasoned leaders rely upon many personal rules developed to simplify running organizations and detecting anomalies in an extremely complex environment. So had Mr. Tata. Simplification is one of the atomic action strategies that is most often used. However, it is not only action but space and time axes too, that provide for developing such approaches. As we will see time strategies correspond to managing speed, rhythm and opportunities, space strategies correspond to effective deployment of resources, fire power and staying power, while action strategies correspond to driving innovation, sustenance and simplification. Thus, multiple alternate mechanisms are available on the STA triangles to achieve similar outcomes albeit with different approaches, risk tolerance and a specific situation. For example, disruption need not only be through innovation, which is an action strategy and frequently deployed by the smaller organizations to disrupt the bigger ones. Mahatma Gandhi used non-cooperation and non-violence as a mechanism to completely disrupt the rhythm of functioning of the state under the British rule – thus utilizing a time strategy to disrupt the stronger one. Of course, the strong use excessive resources at their disposal to attack the competition; they use space strategies. But then there is more to an organization than just deploying disruption.

2.1 Time – The Creator of Experience

Time signifies *a sequence of endless experiences that are definitive*. The experience, positive or negative, is predicated on action and sometimes, inaction. Time is unidirectional, unrepeatable and irreversible, and the relationship of sequence is embedded in every change. Time thus stores value that needs to be realized – action catalyzes this. *Although time is itself unrepeatable, the experiences within it are repeatable.* And it is this cyclical nature of experiences within time that allows us to draw patterns and deduce the likely probability of future outcomes; the linear passage of time quantifies its measure.

The ***time axis*** on the strategy triangles, thus, represents two simultaneously occurring but distinct motions – its own, which is irreversibly sequential and uncontrollable; and the experiences within it that are habitually cyclical. The *unidirectional flow of time* relates to the speed of completion of a task (i.e., its throughput and efficiency). The *cyclical motion* corresponds to the management of business and business cycles and the planning of future outcomes. The *experiences* are nothing but events, and they mark time. The quality of engagement of the actors within the event and the resultant outcome defines the quality of experience. Better experiences usually result in better outcomes. The collective impact of better utilization of unidirectional flow of time, better planning of the cyclical occurrences and improving the quality of experiences within it are the key dimensions of time that we are interested in.

Time encapsulates value, and organizations are driven by *goals* to unlock this value. Goals evolve from the higher *purpose* that underpins one's existence. Achieving goals implies value creation or realizing the coveted end state. Over time goals change; these changes reflect the degree of outcomes achieved or unachieved. The change also reflects the degree of relevance of these goals in a changed environment. *Goals* thus are milestones planned across the future passage of time, while *outcomes are the corresponding* measures that quantify the extent of achievement (or under-achievement) of that plan. Goals are usually distributed across the horizon of decision-making – immediate, mid-term or long-term, in line with achieving the envisioned future. The outcomes need to be carefully chosen for it to be orchestrated and achieved.

Nature has more elements that induce disorder than stability, and if something is left to itself it *will* degrade over time. This is due to the law of increasing entropy. Nature itself is likely akin to a large, complex mathematical model with an infinite number of perturbations capable of spiraling it out of control and making the model unstable. It has a unique penchant for introducing variables that injects change and induces uncertainty. Take earth as an example. The fact that the earth's axis is tilted, and its orbit elliptical (with a minor eccentricity), causes varying day and night, land and sea breeze, and different seasons. But scientists believe that the earth's axial tilt – the eccentricity of its orbit, and, the precession of its axis, all vary over time, albeit over very large cadences in the region of a hundred thousand years or more. Such large periodic changes have highly pronounced effects on earth's climate – and swings between ice ages and warm climates over a period of a-hundred-thousand years. Nature thus relies on a rhythm or periodicity to mark time. Losing rhythm thus indicates chaos.

In all living organisms – plants, animals and human beings, specific genes help to anticipate and respond to daily changes in environment. This internal 'biological clock' that helps us to adapt physiologically to these fluctuations during the day, also known as the *circadian rhythm*, is encoded within our genes and closely synchronized with the earth's revolution. For example, the best time of the day suited for greatest coordination and fastest reaction times, surprisingly, is between 2 and 3 pm in the afternoon! Likewise, the circadian rhythm helps us, to regulate sleep when it is past midnight or keep the body at the highest level of alertness at 9 in the morning. This also explains why jetlag due to travel across time zone needs passage of time before the body adapts to the new time zone.

Nature thus has genetically encoded within all living beings, what we loosely refer to as psyche or natural instinct, to perform daily physical body functions by tying them to its own oscillatory cycles. It has also hard-coded best prescribed times where physical and cerebral actions have the maximum odds of succeeding. *Time, thus, not only stores value that needs to be unlocked via positive experiences, but if the action is timed well with a naturally occurring rhythm, it improves its chance of a successful outcome*. This is true for business and economic cycles as they too behave like living organisms.

The *business cycle*, a key time characteristic, represents a cyclical experience that swings endlessly between the best and the worst of times. It reflects the continuous equilibrium between consumption and production and embodies the sentiment of the economy fluctuating between the states of contraction (or recession), stability (steady) and expansion (growth). If there is an external stimulus, which is most critical for initiating short-term adjustments to a firm's overall strategy – from being conservative to aggressive or vice-versa – then it is triggered with the changes in the business cycle. To soften the ill-effects of the business cycle or to accelerate its good-effects, governments often make the use of monetary policy. The time axis may also represent an individual firm's extraordinary or sub-ordinary state. For example, a start-up with a billion dollars of fund infusion will represent high growth for the firm.

It is impossible to predict and ride a business cycle – sometimes the bust could be triggered by large-scale home loan defaults impacting not only the lending banks but also institutions actively trading in large quantities of dubious quality securitized home loans with a cascading effect. Likewise, recovery could be triggered by governments bailing out businesses or simply due to pent up demand.

However, there are three key levers that help in controlling the impact of business cycle – *resource allocation, risk allocation* and *operational efficiency*. Resource allocation – of people, capital or physical assets, whether owned or aggregated, is the most vital element that needs to be balanced and prioritized between competing needs of today and tomorrow. The choice of building capacity in advance of a projected increase in demand or increasing the sales capacity, lies within the domain of resource allocation. The goal is to maximize return on investment for all the stake holders. Constant portfolio review for prioritization and rationalization during business planning cycles, keeps resource allocation aligned to strategic objectives of the firm usually allocated to functions, products and programs.

Risk diversification is the second powerful lever and a potent antidote during downturns. Risk diversification is the allocation of resources in such a fashion that it reduces the exposure of downside carried by any single class of asset to controllable limits. Risk management can be achieved by spreading or allocating risk both across a portfolio of projects and across multiple shareholders.

The last lever, efficiency, focuses on all operational, financial and organizational metrics and the continued effort to drive them up. It is the continuous effort of being able to do more in less time. While the first two need to be reviewed and optimized based on the state of the business cycle, good companies constantly look at ways to improve efficiency in everything that they do. In each of these, the question that needs to be answered is – how much are we willing to invest in tomorrow, or sacrifice it, in a bid to sustain today?

Leaders apply these three levers in varying combinations. Some who are highly risk averse and conservative would look at managing the present by striving for higher than normal efficiency and by controlling what they can – costs. Thus, profits are the key focus for such leaders. Other leaders, more centered, may reinvest savings achieved from productivity and efficiency improvements into investments for tomorrow. There could yet be a very few highly aggressive and radical leaders who could adopt the risky path of enormous investments for the future even during troubled times, and either risk plummeting the firm into nothingness or emerge as far-sighted, fearless leaders who led their firms to stellar heights. But here is a simple view – if the investment is to fill a discontinuity that the environment has presented, it is always advantageous to plow right ahead and not lose momentum, the signature moves of Elon Musk. Alternatively, the capital commitments could be made in smaller chunks and reviewed at shorter intervals unless earmarked for long strategic programs. The size of the firm matters too – a small start-up probably needs to rely on better risk allocation or seek investors through equity dilution to help fuel business momentum and reduce risk of existence. On the contrary, larger companies need to learn how to be nimble by driving better efficiencies and resorting to correct resource allocation to reduce the risk of losing their customers. The medium -size companies have the most flexibility as they can act a bit of both. Any investor money should be only for expansion of business, investment in tomorrow's offerings or for the need to support growth and increased operating expenses but at lower cost of capital.

*

When the three levers are not managed well the results can be devastating. One of the biggest reasons for companies collapsing is due to ignorance of the virtues of 'risk allocation' and risk management. Firms border on risky behavior initially considering them to be outliers only; but if those decisions begin to give disproportionate returns, firms tend to become brave and amalgamate such behavior into main-stream strategy. One stark example was the sub-prime crisis in 2008, which was a direct outcome of ignoring the edicts of 'risk allocation' and banks having a very high proportion of sub-prime borrowers. Risk allocation becomes more acute when firms are operating in high-risk environments such as molecular research or biotech funds where 95% of drug trials fail. The best outcome can then be a function of the normal distribution curve and the worst, a complete wipe out. However, Deep Knowledge Ventures (DKV), a Hong Kong-based biotechnology venture capital fund, chose a novel method to apply the rigor of risk allocation to its decision-making. While a raging debate continues about whether machines will become smarter than humans, DKV has successfully harnessed the intelligence of such machines. Way back in 2014, DKV inducted a robot, VITAL, on its board with full voting rights. Dmitry Kaminskiy, Managing Partner of DKV, maintains that they would have definitely gone belly up in such a volatile space, but for VITAL. He also reckons that the larger the data set, the better is the robot's decision-making capability and hence VITAL's recommendations have become better over time. The company is now underway releasing the next version of its board member, VITAL2, to replace VITAL. Dmitry also believes that "decentralized autonomous intelligent companies" with the capability of driving business decisions that are significantly better in managing business risks, even without any human intervention, is not too far off.

Another example is a British Independent Software Product Vendor (ISV), which misapplied resource allocation and met with a similar fate. With every customer acquisition came a lot of customer requested features that the company was willing to deliver at a subsidized additional price. The result – although the ISV was building additional customized features for the customer, it was accounting the costs under the general product, and provisioning it as capital expenditure (or IP, with capital expenditure depreciation over time), instead of expensing it and charging it fully to the customer account. Otherwise, it would have shown the customer accounts in loss. The profit and loss accounts for the year, of course, looked great but deteriorated over time as more customers were acquired using the same strategy. A company once adored on the equity bourses became a single-digit penny stock.

A remarkable example of operationalization efficiency is Reliance Industries in India, which was steadfast in its approach to set up the world's largest petroleum refinery at Jamnagar in less than three years despite being told by the best in the business that anything less than five years would not be possible. They brilliantly saved time and hence costs too.

Jamnagar is a city in the western part of India. To save time, Reliance commissioned ships on which not only parts of the plant were being transported but were simultaneously assembled while *en route*. Jamnagar had only a small inland port, where large ships could not dock. It thus needed a jetty, miles into the sea, for offloading the large assembled parts from the ships that were carrying them. A jetty was built. Large trucks were imported, which could carry the sub-assembled parts of the plant inland. The whole senior management camped in Jamnagar, closely directing the operations and the result was Jamnagar refinery getting commissioned in two years and eight months flat. Reliance had viewed the passive transportation of the plant and machinery on a ship as waste and converted that into the active cycle of plant assembly on the moving ship itself. For Reliance, operationalization efficiency and the quick commissioning the plant was of paramount importance, and they controlled it aggressively to avoid any unnecessary commissioning costs being listed on the balance sheet (operationalization of a plant is accounted in the balance sheet as assets).

*

Table 2.1 below captures examples of time strategies that organizations of various categories typically adopt while going through recession, stable or growth in business cycles.

2.2 Space – The Essence of Boundary

Space signifies *co-existence, boundary, resistance or experience of force.* A physical point in space can be represented by coordinates along the x, y and z axes. Any

Table 2.1 Summary of Time Strategies during Recession, Stable and Growth Cycles of Start-up, Medium and Large Organizations

	Market Timing	Recession	Stable	Growth
Time Levers	Resource Allocation	Tight	Liberal	Experimentational
	Risk Allocation	Highly controlled	Conservative portfolio	Aggressive portfolio
	Efficiency	Very high	Balanced	Relaxed
Organization Types	Start-ups	Preserve capital	Operationalize and sell	Commit new features, customized deliveries, sell to larger firm in similar space
		Market product before it is ready	Exit strategy to cash out especially when not well differentiated	
	Medium	Maintain margins	Increase market share	Increase capacities
		Preserve costs	Expand customer base, increase R&D spend, allied services	
	Large organizations	Maintain margins and market share. Centralize decision-making and cut costs	Increase capacity, increase R&D spend	Invest into new areas and customers; No. 1 or 2 market position

other point in its proximity can be represented by the coordinates of yet another unique co-existing position. Space extends infinitely in all directions but can be limited in area by a set of imaginary lines and/or planes. Such limits create bounded space or space boundaries. Space is deemed to be empty unless occupied by matter. When space is occupied by matter it can be perceived through touch and its presence is felt due to the resistance offered by it when touched. Resistance also implies competition in business context. Crowded market spaces are sometimes referred to as red-ocean while unoccupied market spaces are referred to as blue-oceans. *Thus, any experience within space is an experience of force – either exerting or being exerted upon. Managing space is part of business well-being.*

Space could also be non-physical (i.e., mind – both conscious and sub-conscious). When conscious mind-space is occupied by thoughts, the outputs manifest as emotions or reasoning. The conscious mind constantly grapples between learnings of the past and the outcomes desired in the future. Understanding consumer mind-space is critical to a firm's success. The sub-conscious mind-space is subtler and lies well outside the domain of the current text. Managing mind-space is part of emotional well-being and will be touched upon where ever necessary.

The *space axis* on the strategy triangles, represents the overall market and the *territory* within which the business operates; it also represents the mind of the consumer. A lot has been written on space and its control, especially in the conflicts of war and competition in the markets. The most important element in winning a war is in choosing one's battles carefully. The choice of terrain is key, as is understanding the lay of the land, the escape routes and the strategic positions, all of which combine to give a winning advantage. Likewise, in a competitive business, the space or the territorial axis denotes both the total market and the competitive arena of influence that a firm operates in. Any competitive space can be divided into three well demarcated sub-territories – *own, known and unknown.*

Owned market spaces correspond to stronghold market segments, which are well understood or offer maximum opportunities to a firm, also known as its addressable market; it is the sub-segment that the firm thrives in. Owned territory is deeply understood in terms of its contours, customer needs and a well-fitting solution that is likely to generate most of the company's revenues and profits.

'Known' refers to market spaces that are adjacent and have either not actively been pursued or are accessed via alliances. Known segments are secondary competitive spaces that generate much smaller chunks of revenue for a firm and a competitor has a much superior control over this space; but this segment is not completely out-of-interest. Firms want to play in these adjacent sub-segments not only to extend their reach but also to engage with the competition, which if left unchecked, may breach and even wrest control of the firm's owned territories.

Finally, 'unknown' markets are sub-segments not always well understood or of major interest to a firm and hence usually ignored. Unknown territories are also those in which the competition matters little or is irrelevant in the foreseeable future. Interest usually spurs in this sub-segment because of an unrelated asset base or a sudden opening of opportunities (e.g., a firm sitting on large land banks may lean towards housing as a business if it is shutting down polluting factories from city areas; or the sudden spurt in use of digital payment providers post the currency demonetization in India). Most disruptive technology start-ups have exploited this space as an entry point to launch their ventures and have generated huge valuations and competitive leverage; one such example is the swift rise of the PayTM period during the currency demonetization in India.

As the space axis represents both the total market size and consumer needs, it helps the firm in demarcating its *addressable market.* A business plan assumes that a firm has a set of services or products that customers within its addressable market space are willing to consume at a price where the firm will make reasonable profits in the long run. This also helps the firm to determine the specifics around customer acquisitions, product and service innovations, market expansions, etc., to name a few.

War strategists have constantly opined that for the established, the best form of offense is defense, primarily because one waits for the enemy entrenched in one's stronghold. Of course, if under-prepared, the enemy can inflict debilitating damage. *Defense, attack and alliances* are three *space moves* that map to business territorial strategies too. The primary strategy is to firmly defend owned spaces. For managing known spaces either the flanges where the segment domination by the competition is weak should be attacked as direct attack is usually expensive and destructive in such situations, or, one must rely upon alliances. Alliance could be predicated upon common or supplementary strengths of the collaborating firms wanting to achieve scale; or in another form, firms could harmonize complementary strengths to forward or backward integrate within the same segment. Finally, using direct and indirect attack, and/or surprise, would be the recommended way to enter unknown spaces, maintain the experts. Regardless, successful space maneuvers are always dependent upon understanding 'enemy' weaknesses, systematically breaking down their assumptions and effective deployment of own limited resources.

Start-ups disrupting traditional firms is largely about space strategies. Amazon used ecommerce to disrupt traditional firms globally but were finding it difficult to breach the Indian market due to a hardened buyer mindset of not using credit or debit cards for online payments – the urban population feared online frauds while the rural population did not have this power. When Sachin and Binny Bansal started their ecommerce venture, Flipkart, in 2008 in India after quitting their jobs at Amazon, they knew that for their venture to succeed they needed to make payment modalities less complicated. The Bansals knew they needed to somehow facilitate payments at the time of delivery and not at the time of accepting the order. They innovated the simple 'cash-on-delivery' mechanism, the key reason why ecommerce platforms became even viable and later extremely popular in India. Simplifying customer experience by overcoming customer mind-blocks allowed them to get to the number one slot rapidly. Flipkart used space and offense with better ammunition to combat the market entry. Fast-forward ten years, today payments have advanced to contactless car keys, wearables like watches and research now at the dawn of enabling retina scans or chips embedded in the palm or nails to trigger this; it ceases to be an advantage anymore, but the ease of usage even today remains an important area of research.

Space moves also are visible when the big firms are threatened. Alliance as a display of power is constantly adopted by the disrupted or those likely to be disrupted in the form of consortiums. Blockchain as a technology threatens to steamroll the way cross-border payments will be made in future and the steep commissions that currency intermediaries will be able to charge. Libra is one such consortium founded by Facebook and has many payment organizations as part of the group; of course, if successful it will disrupt a lot of existing players – big and small, but this is an instance of how the big firms strike back. Flipkart could not sustain the might of Amazon's fire power in India and decided to exit after selling the firm to Walmart.

Leaders adopt the three space moves – defense, alliance and attack, in varying combinations. A *competitive leader* bases his approach on efficient market theory and its consequence that information is freely available to all. They rely upon the tenets of a running concern, differentiation and innovation as the core to battle in the marketplace. The *collaborative leader* relies upon partnering as the means to battle in the market; collaboration is always among equals or between entities having complementary strengths. NGOs, acquisitions to expand customer base or to acquire complementary competencies, creating joint Intellectual Properties (IPs) and private–public partnerships are key examples of how collaborative leaders approach engagement in the market. The *combative leader* uses the theory of war and hostility as the means to battle in the market; however, there must not always be a negative connotation to this approach. Hostile acquisitions, launching a highly commoditized or competitive product with cut-throat strategies or even open source movements are some scenarios where combative leadership style excels well. Combative leaders usually like to annihilate all competition whenever they decide to enter the market and always have a superior strength of resources at their disposal. Though leaders use a combination of all three leadership-action styles from their arsenal based on the situation they are facing, they usually have a dominant leadership-style that they naturally gravitate towards.

Every business concern must necessarily adopt a competitive approach when operating in a market. This means price, innovation and differentiation is continuously critical for survival of the business. The last few decades of strategy evolution has seen this aplenty and traditional companies like GE, IBM, Ford, Airbus and the like have understood, mastered and implemented this within the veins of their organizations. They continuously ride the cycle of being at their very best and then not necessarily being at their very best. Each time they touch a low, they device a new strategy that is in consonance with changed times and customer needs, which propels them back up again. They undergo transformations, which is the cycle of 'death of the irrelevant followed by the creation of the new and relevant.'

Transformations are discussed in detail later. Time and again, organizations need to go through this continuous cycle or perish.

The combative leaders adopt a very aggressive stance, possible, due to the immense strength they derive from disproportionate and abundant resources at their disposal. A great example is Reliance-Jio Telecom, in India, which has invested heavily into a sector that was ailing; however, the aggressiveness of their pricing and the product bundle that they offered made them the single largest telecom company in India within a year of their launch beating their local and global rivals entrenched in the business for ages. Many start-ups, who have made their fortunes either on the bourses or by diluting their holdings, are now themselves in the race for investing into the future potential unicorns. Unlike traditional companies, these tech companies compete on future disruption, something they themselves have done earlier but may not be in position to do that continuously. Alibaba, Amazon, Facebook and Google have invested in a wide array of diverse companies, which are working to get answers relevant to the oncoming future.

With the neo-tech firms leading true innovation, traditional technology services companies like IBM and Microsoft have taken a supporting and collaborative role. They work with key customers to help create newer and path-breaking solutions, something that they previously did on their own. This is due to the shift to 'attitudinal economics' as pure technology may not be deemed to be a competitive advantage but just an enabler. This is discussed later in the book.

Table 2.2 summarizes the above discussion with examples of how space strategy can be applied to various product and service types.

Table 2.2 Application of Space Strategies to Various Products and Services Types

Space		Own	Known	Unknown	Examples
Strategy		Defend	Flange attack/alliance	Direct or Indirect attack	
Product Type	*Campaign Objective*	Levers			
Premium	Ownership	Snob value, especially crafted	Kitting	Accessories	Ferrari, Manchester United
	Subscription	Privileges and discounts	Sudden discount windows, starter/monthly packs	Special subscriber events, periodic changes	Amazon Prime, Your Green Canvas
Durables	Replacement	Price, feature, brand	Specialized companies, exchange	Support sales via turnkey projects or leasing; land banks and asset strength	GE, TV and car manufacturers
Consumables	Annuity	Continuous feature enhancements, cost reduction	Product convergence, substitution and extension	Platforms	Apple, Reliance Jio

2.3 Action – The Force that Alters Boundaries and Experiences

The *action axis* on the strategy triangles, signifies a force that helps in creating or altering experiences and boundaries. Thus, the action axis signifies either an initiation of an action or a response to a stimulus.

Recapitulating, *action*, manifests only in three primary value-generating modes – addition, amendment and deletion – analogous to creation, sustenance and destruction/ simplification). Primary actions are those that make changes to the current state. There is one non-primary but a compound action that is often used by leaders and was introduced earlier – transformations. There is one other non-primary activity that does not alter any state but is used for feedback and that is 'inquiry' or 'reporting.'

Creation signifies birth – of a brand, a start-up, a product, a service or an intent. In a competitive setting, this indicates throwing a challenge to the existing players or alternatively, carving out a small niche for a specific segment of customers. Creation could also be aggregation – for example, Airbnb did not buy assets but used the aggregated unused room at homes as a virtual hotel inventory to fulfill traveler demand.

'Sustenance' signifies running an enterprise or an operation not only without degradation, but, with constant improvement. Customer choices evolve over time, assets degrade, costs and competition increase in intensity and in general, customers demand more for less. This fundamental variable focusses on delivering the stakeholders' expectations.

Deletion, destruction or simplification signifies end-of-life. Retiring assets, sale of stake, removing lower priority items, consolidation and pulling a product out of the market, are examples of 'deletion.' Likewise, organizational and financial restructuring, harmonization of efforts, removal of duplication and centralization vs. decentralization, are all matters related to simplification.

The action axis represents lifecycle. A *lifecycle* is the identification of key stages in the life of an inanimate or an animate object, the most characteristic being the human lifecycle – of birth-growth-and-death; every being goes through these three stages; however, there are an infinite combination of passages to choose from, which finally determines the quantum of success and the degree of satisfaction the person derives from their life. Likewise, all products that a firm sells go through an engineering design lifecycle, and the services through a service design lifecycle. Firms too traverse through a similar lifecycle. A lifecycle thus has tasks or activities laid out with well-intentioned outcomes defined at the end of each task. It does not, however, impose any rigid time boundary for completion of a specific task or the entire process. The quality of decisions taken in selecting from the alternative paths available at each of the sub-stages of the lifecycle determines the quality of outcomes at each of those sub-stages, and hence, at the overall level. It is thus the quality of decision-making that determines the quality of outcome.

Usually, in an extremely complex business environment, the leader does not have the liberty of assuming just one of the three roles in isolation. He must be all three amalgamated into one and donning them to partly initiate new and/or disruptive ideas and strategies, partly to sustain and grow the existing and partly to terminate the old. This is necessitated to sustain the core of the enterprise and terminate or transform the old, the norm or the obsolete. One such apt example who used these three roles to perfection was Steve Jobs. Jobs had the fearlessness of killing his best-selling products before his competitors could do so. He discontinued the products when they were at their peak and either merged the specs of those best-selling products into a brand-new product (like merging the specs of the iPod into the iPhone) or significantly improved that product to something dramatically new (every version of iPhone). Jobs was a *transformational leader* who operated more as a combination of destroyer–creator, which can be seen from the many innovative Apple products that were launched in the last three decades but only a handful of them that remain in current production.

The *innovation-led* leaders are those who continuously churn out great new products and services. They are the growth leaders who can ratchet up sales year on year. Alibaba and Amazon are prolific examples of such leadership too.

Bill Gates, on the other hand, uses the combination of the three actions biased more towards using *investment-led sustenance* leadership. Microsoft has created fewer product genres than Apple, as well as an even smaller number of truly transformational upgrades and releases of its operating systems. Today, they are increasingly supporting their customers as a collaborative partner, while they continue their research in their own chosen areas.

Of course, as a grim reminder, the most difficult role to perform is that of the preserver because it is almost impossible to preserve anything in permanence. Time operates like a destroyer and the creator needs to continually keep giving birth to new ways. Sustenance thus is a continuous battle of survival and innovation. Standing still is never an option.

Finally, the *improvement or simplification leaders* are the classic turnaround specialists who know how to simplify an organization – as the first step by cutting costs, rooting out duplications and reorganizing to drive economies of scale, and then, driving growth and expansion as the next logical step.

*

The combination of three actions in determining the final execution path is not only limited to the products of a company but also to its business and/or management models, the space it operates in, the people and its ultimate goals. Table 2.3 is an example of how time-space equivalent

Table 2.3 Action Strategies vis-à-vis Time–Space Equivalence

Action Strategies		Create	Sustain	Reduce
Combined Time–Space Equivalence	Risk + attack	Expansion vs. upward/downward integration	Acquire vs. build strengthen vs diversify	Core vs. context, dilute vs invest
	Resource + alliance	Buy vs. make	Invest in new areas vs expand in existing	Divest vs. hold
	Efficiency + defend	Upgrading vs. replacing	Restructuring vs. rightsizing	Multiskilling vs. downsizing

strategies can be combined with action levers to arrive at appropriate organizational strategies.

2.4 In Summary

- *Time* signifies experience, space signifies boundary and hence strength, while action signifies force that alters both experience as well as boundary.
- Time encapsulates value and organizations are driven by goals to unlock this. It thus represents opportunity.
- Goals and outcomes are milestones that mark the passage of time – it compares the planned intent to the achieved results.
- Time traces the business cycle; business cycle can be managed via resource allocation, risk allocation and operational efficiency.
- Three types of time leaders
  - Risk averse, focus on the present and manage efficiency and costs. Profit motive.
  - Invest savings into the business of tomorrow. Balance between growth and profits.
  - High risk appetite. Invest in the business of the future by filling up a discontinuity.
- *Space* defines the overall market and the addressable sub-markets within it.
- Owned spaces correspond to stronghold market segments, known spaces correspond to adjacent sub-segments and unknown spaces may not be of immediate interest to a firm.
- Firms usually defend owned spaces, use alliance for known spaces and attack to annex unknown spaces.
- Three types of space leaders
  - Competitive – use tenets of running concern, differentiation and innovation. Conforms to efficient market theory.

- Collaborative – relies upon partnering as means to battle in the market. Among equals.
- Combative leader – relies upon war and hostility. Endowed with some exceptional strength.
- *Action* generates value.
- There are three primary value-generating actions – create, preserve and destroy. Destruction is analogous to simplification. Transformation is a complex action.
- Four types of action leaders
  - Transformation led – kill their best products before competition does so.
  - Innovation led – create great new products and services; usually growth leaders.
  - Improvement led – Innovation for sustenance for products that stays long enough.
  - Simplification led – usually turnaround leaders.
- Action represents lifecycle of a being.

Chapter 3

Chapter 3

Integrating Time, Space and Action

Charting Pathways to Successful Outcomes

It was in 1987 when the celebrity chef Hemant Oberoi opened The Zodiac Grill on the fourth floor of the Taj Mahal Hotel at Apollo Bunder in Mumbai. The Grill was fashioned for the epicures and the cognoscenti as a luxurious, fine-dining restaurant, with its menu boasting a selection of caviars, escargots, sea-food and the most delicate wines, to name a few. The Grill was truly well-appointed with Christofle plates from Paris, Riedel glassware and decanters from Austria, and its initial uniforms from London's Simon Jersey. But there was a twist – the menu card had nothing on its right-hand side. Way back in 1987, when India was grappling with its fragile finances, the Tatas had gambled with a 'pay-what-you-want' format for a very high-end restaurant. The debatable question – could the restaurant make money, or would it be a wash out?

In March 2017, Elon Musk announced his ambitious project, Neuralink, to build a high-bandwidth, minimally invasive human brain machine interface, so that humans could keep continually ahead of the machines in the wake of their rapidly increasing intelligence. Neuralink also came with the promise of treating people with healthcare conditions emanating from impaired brain functions via a simple brain implant. The same debatable question – will this work?

3.1 Areas Bounded by Two Adjacent Fundamental Axes

Space, time and action can be combined in pairs to produce three extremely powerful views, very useful in strategy evaluation, its planning and its execution. This interplay gives rise to time–space, space–action and time–action dimensions that can respectively help align a firm its strengths to opportunities, build a strong competitive advantage via appropriate market-engagement options and help in adopting a suitable producer–consumer relationship approach – supply side, demand side or attitudinal economics. Attitudinal economics transcends the conventional economic approach as will be seen in this chapter and which Oberoi in our first example applied; the result was outrageously successful. The tools discussed in this chapter can help in drilling down into key areas of business impact with the potential choice of actions available. Each of these has its own standalone sphere of influence and can be used in discrete analysis of business factors across these three different dimensions. Such outputs can then become inputs to fine-tuning the overall strategy.

3.2 The Time–Space Dimension – Matching Opportunities to Strengths

A firm's primary objective is to exploit opportunities; commercial firms exploit commercial opportunities and discontinuities in the market. If there were no opportunities, howsoever obscure, there would be no firms. Opportunities arise from needs. Just as needs evolve over time, opportunities evolve over time too. Needs get commoditized over time and the competition fiercer. Thus, managing costs, profits and growth to sustain and grow market share becomes the core tenet of managing the 'business of today.'

Firms expand customer needs by expanding their product features and invading the boundaries of their competition and adjacent spaces. They integrate horizontally or vertically to increase their product footprint to vie for bigger share of their customers' wallet. This warrants strategic investments, a key step in expanding into the 'business of tomorrow.'

There exists yet another breed of entrepreneurs – the disruptors or the dreamers, who give no credence to the background or industry expertise they want to disrupt. Their strategy – to evaluate every assumption that the industry bases itself upon and breaking them down systematically to create a new paradigm and challenge the long entrenched traditional incumbents. They look at resources that can risk the competitors' sustainability (sometimes even life itself on this planet); their task, to make such scarce resources either abundantly available or create alternatives for them. The former needs knowledge, critical thinking and experimentation while the latter need all above and a large amount of funds for sustained breakthrough innovation testing. These disruptors create the 'businesses of the future.' Elon Musk is one such example.

Opportunities and threats are two sides of the same coin – what one sees as a threat, another may see the same as an opportunity. Unearthing opportunities and threats to take advantage from them remains a critical function of any business strategy. The approaches to strategizing the business of today, tomorrow and the future are different because the first two rely on market data, market benchmarks and view of the world, while the latter is based on gut, experimentation, speed and personal view of the future with varying or no industry insight on the same. However, there is always some method to the madness.

The *time–space* dimension is a powerful tool that can help a firm align itself to exploit opportunities best suited to its strengths for the business of today and tomorrow and help identify and manage weaknesses and threats in the short term. It also helps in identifying the business of the future by aligning and exploiting long-term threats as disruptive opportunities.

For managing the business of today and tomorrow, all strategic assessment is firmly predicated on understanding the age-old work horse, the organizational SWOT (i.e., its strengths, weaknesses, threats and opportunities). The threats are evaluated on a three to five-year horizon. Companies don't necessarily venture beyond this period for their business planning. To avoid becoming blindsided by the impending future, which could be very different and disruptive, 'futurists' are usually involved in strategy sessions. Mostly the will of the organization is more focused on the immediate, short and the medium terms than the future that is ten to 15 years out. They neither understand the receiving future generation nor their likely needs. Thus, the futurist's session, though critical, remains on paper. In short, there is no 'budget for failure' for evaluating future alternatives. There is one other reason too to look at such long terms – the law of scaling.

Geoff West, a renowned British theoretical physicist and distinguished professor of Santa Fe Institute, New Mexico, applied the laws of Physics to Biology and unearthed some unbelievably simple correlations in scaling. He noticed, as the size of living creatures increased, the amount of additional energy needed to maintain the extra body weight, increased in a ratio that was sub linear (i.e., if a 75 kg living being needed 2000 calories every day for it to survive, then a 150 kg living being did not need 4000 calories but only 3400). The economies of scale being exhibited meant that as size increased from one lifeform to another, the biology in keeping the bigger lifeforms alive become more and more efficient. He used many other metrics like number of heartbeats per lifetime, etc., to confirm his findings.

West also found that companies and cities too behaved quite like living beings in scaling, but with one strong difference between them. While companies exhibited sub-linear scaling or economies of scale, the cities exhibited a super-linear scaling or increasing returns to scale. This means while cities are self-energizing and can never die, companies, like living organisms, have only a certain life span and must die.

The scaling law, postulating sub-linear scaling with growth of a company and implying economies of scale, is both good and bad. While it shows a terrific correlation to efficient operations with growth, and hence better returns, it also reminds that firms have a finite life. Hence investments and planned transformations are a must, as like every other living being, all companies must die and only transformations will allow it to be reborn again. In short, if there is "no budget for failure," a favorite quote from the futurist, Anton Musgrave, it truly is end-of-life for the organizations.

Since short-term strategy usually involves matching of immediate strengths to immediate opportunities within owned spaces, both strengths and opportunities needs to be well understood. Unfortunately, both tend to be over-exaggerated. Countless business strategies are based on the flawed assumption of large addressable market size and the potential of the firm (in reality – any firm) to corner a small part of it; what they overlook is lack of any compelling strength that positions the firm well enough to exploit the available opportunity. The test of a truly differentiated strength is the rapid pace at which a firm's revenue can likely increase or the rate at which it can acquire and retain customers.

It is not always easy to spot threats and opportunities as many a time opportunities present themselves in the form of an adversity; many a time an impending threat of disruption either gets camouflaged by the insignificance of a challenger's size or gets submerged under the ego of an established brand. The strengths could be in a differentiated product (or lower price of production, better brand name, eye-popping service levels, lower price through aggregation, removal of intermediaries, etc.), while the opportunities could lie unexposed due to a discontinuity in a highly specific customer segment, or the lack of confidence to disrupt an existing market, or just due to unmanageable expanding market conditions. In the medium- to long-term, managing non-immediate but potential threats and weaknesses, or evaluating opportunities that may look unlikely today but could be the cornerstones in the future (e.g., solar power replacing fossil fuel-driven power). The overall approach itself lends into devising a downstream execution plan.

The external state of the business cycle ('time' characteristics) and the firm's strengths and appetite for its footprint in specific territorial boundaries ('space' characteristics) determines the potential choices available to a firm. The time dimension corresponds to contraction, steady and growth strategies while the space dimensions corresponds to own, known and unknown strategies.

Combining the two dimensions above, on the basis of the time–space demarcations, likely strategies that emerge along the 'contraction–own,' 'steady–known' and 'growth–unknown' sub-segments are to *exploit* opportunities in owned spaces, *explore* opportunities in known spaces but *explode* opportunities in unknown spaces, respectively. If explosive opportunities don't exist in unknown spaces, there must be other reasons (e.g., human deliverance to pursue such paths). Since the risk quotient of the strategy increases from left to right on the strategy triangle, the upside from opportunities in the rightmost unknown space should be truly enormous; thus, the timing of market entry or assistance from the business cycle or a sudden discontinuity in the environment can provide large windfall of opportunities.

The strength of a successful organization is a function of its capabilities and customer loyalty in its strong hold or its addressable markets, and by definition, should be well exploited. Thus, the 'contraction-own' or 'the business of today,' is based on the 'OWN STRENGTHS' operative position of an organization. It is important to note that all opportunities within its owned spaces must be exploited before significant capital is moved to be invested outside of this zone. This is also the zone to firmly defend. During market contraction or when faced with undue internal challenges, most firms use transformation and simplification to reinvent themselves.

The 'steady–known' sub-segment, also 'the business of tomorrow' presents the widest array of opportunities to any firm that wants to expand. This is based on 'LEVERAGED and SUPPLEMENTARY STRENGTHS' operative position of the firm. Firms use alliance to sell some of its core offerings into such adjacent spaces – the pivot being general understanding of the space by the firms but with the need for a partner to understand region specific nuances or to gain access. Firms use marginal costing during their initial or investigation period and once established improve prices and margins. The expansion into known spaces is best when a business is in a steady state and there are no likely impending shocks that can spook the market, although this condition may not always be guaranteed. Firms also use vertical and horizontal integration to effortlessly expand into cross-selling to their existing customers. This is synonymous to deepening their hold or strengthening their control on own and known spaces. Yet another set of global firms sitting on an depreciated item on their balance sheets like prime real-estate in the center of the cities have used it for their expansion into construction, real-estate or allied industry, or, converted inhouse owned large data-centers into commercial cloud ventures.

There is yet another category in the 'business of tomorrow' – when firms want to expand into known spaces without the help of an alliance or going direct (sometimes they acquire a small partner to give a minor head start to themselves). Such strategy moves are akin to 'attack and disrupt,' a move usually deployed for unknown markets. However, the firm sees a similar large-sized opportunity available at a low-cost direct investment. This is a less used strategic move for most firms as although the market is generally understood, space in terms of its constituent competition and statutory constraints has not been directly experienced and hence is in semi-known territory.

And finally, the disruptors view the existing long-term threats for incumbents as their core opportunities. Armed with a preposterous idea to unleash such a threat, 'the business of the future' relies upon breaking down every assumption valid today. In short, they look upon very long-term threats of today as their food for creating the future. The 'growth–unknown' sub-segment represents aggression in support of the businesses of future. This is based on 'DISRUPTIVE STRENGTHS' operative position of the firm. Challenger firms like classic technology start-ups saw huge opportunities to disrupt markets by changing the rules of the game (e.g., by the virtue of aggregation, reuse or the power of platforms). Amazon, Uber, Airbnb, Tesla and SpaceX are the obvious examples, some of which are explained later in the text. Established firms usually experiment with unknown spaces during times of the growth cycle; however, challengers and disruptors press the pedal whenever they spot the discontinuity.

3.3 The Space–Action Dimension – Building Competitive Advantage through Market-engagement Choices

The **space–action** dimension is perhaps the most powerful and yet the simplest of the 'two fundamental variables' interplay to apply. This is also a very superior tool for firms to help identify a mix of effective strategic go-to-market-engagements in building and exploiting competitive advantage. This dimension, closely comparable to fighting a battle or waging a war, is an extremely well researched subject from the ancient times, and equally well documented.

Decades ago, Porter argued that competitive advantage could be built in three ways; cost leadership – providing high quality services at low costs, differentiation – being the best in the category, or, focus – having a category, sub-category or a niche under the organization's control. The obvious corollary is, if organizations cannot differentiate then the only option available to them is being a cost leader. It also implied that both the strategies were not deployable simultaneously. Of course, the latest research in this area now shows that a hybrid strategy is necessary to combat the unpredictability of the markets and the most successful companies have been those who have adopted such a mixed strategy.

Organizations tend to rely on strong differentiation, high risk–reward leverage and disruptive technologies to break away from the ordinary but without taking their eye off the mundane aspects of doing business. One may even buy market share via discounts, but it is the customer stickiness at reasonable profits that changes the fortunes of the company in the long-term. This comes with either differentiation or cost leadership, or both, and firms use a reasonable mix of continuous improvement at one end of the spectrum, innovation in the middle and pure transformation at the other extremity to achieve such objectives.

Many researchers and practitioners have extensively applied war strategies to sales and marketing, most drawing their inspiration from two ageless texts –Sun Tzu's third century BC treatise *The Art of War*, and Clausewitz's eighteenth-century war journal *On War*. As briefly discussed earlier, there are just three basic war moves – attack, alliance and defense, which are the fundamental go-to-market strategies. Professor Vasconcellos, who has extensively researched war moves, and corresponding marketing moves, defines attack as 'entry plus unprovoked' – attack is characterized by a self-initiated and unprovoked movement into a new area (industry, geography, or the way things are done). Defense, on the other hand, is when one of the above two criteria is absent. Thus, a company entering a new market as a response to a competitor is defense but the same move without any provocation is attack. Similarly, 'standstill' or holding one's ground is an act of defense. Standing still but not taking cognizance of the changing competitive environment is one of the key reasons for 'Goliath' falling prey to 'David' and history is replete with such examples – Sony, Kodak, etc. Finally, alliances are used to buy time, speed or strength. Alliance can be strategic and long term or tactical and short term. Both attack and defense strategies can be deployed in building alliance (e.g., acquisition vs. franchising). Many a time large firms competitively engage unlikely small competition via alliances because 'they cannot be ignored' lest they become formidable forces in near future. When SAP was firming its foothold in India, it had fostered its presence even in some of the then tier two cities via alliances and partners. The inherent idea was to engage in competitive bids within the ERP market, even in tier two cities, where buyers were not yet open to buying expensive ERP software. However, it was more to blunt the competition and at the same time build a potential future replacement pipeline, likely when the firm had grown and ready for the next buy. This strategy from SAP together with micro-verticals helped them establish a hugely dominant market share in the sub-continent boasting of some incredibly large as well as a huge number of small deals.

The space dimension corresponds to own, known and unknown strategies while the action dimension corresponds to optimize, preserve and expand strategies. Combining the two dimensions above, basis the space–action demarcations, the most well-established and widely applicable strategies are along *own–optimize, known–preserve and unknown–expand* sub-segments, with actions translating into defense, alliance and attack respectively.

For many organizations, incremental innovation is the norm; however, this part of the story is for only basic survival. Sustained innovation with different objectives across the three sub-segments is needed; Applegate and Harreld correlated similar findings in their research of the IBM turnaround, some of the which are referenced below.

The 'own–optimize' on the space–action sub-segment, focuses on continuously improving the price–value equation. Input costs increase year-on-year usually faster than what the firms can afford to pass on as price increase to the customer. Thus, firms need to continuously re-engineer and optimize to give more at lower costs, true always, but mandatory during bad times. This is thus the *INCREMENTAL INNOVATION and OPERATIONAL IMPROVEMENTS* with direct go-to-market operational position of the firm. In the research paper on how IBM survived during its turnaround period in the 1990s, Applegate and Harreld termed this as 'surviving the market.'

The 'known–preserve' presents the widest array of possibilities to any firm that wants to thrive and expand. Firms lose steam in growth businesses over time and sustainability remains a threat. Firms adopt the route of innovating new products for existing markets, or that of acquisitions to extend its customer base and its offerings, or, even expand into adjacent markets either directly or through partners. This position is based on leveraged differentiation as well as strategic positioning. Sometimes the firms can be different in different markets too, to retain the same competitive advantage. Thus, this is the *STRATEGIC INNOVATION and SUSTAINABILITY* go-to-market operative position. This has been described by Applegate and Harreld as 'thriving the market.'

An exponential extension can be applied to the 'unknown–expand' sub-segment that represents aggression and unusual annexation. Firms see huge opportunities based on solid differentiation and the way they solve a problem. Usually the technology used is highly disruptive to the core tenets of doing business in that industry and the approach is untapped leverage and aggregation rather than huge investments. Sometimes companies release valuable assets they are sitting on to achieve this. Thus, this is the *BREAKTHROUGH INNOVATION and DISRUPTIVE* go-to-market operative position of the firm; this is also the author's extension of Applegate and Harreld's research and he calls this 'driving the market.' This is highly transformative in nature.

3.4 The Time–Action Dimension – Enhancing Experiences via Supply Side, Demand Side and Attitudinal Economics

Among other things, one of the objectives of a commercial firm is to sell and make profits. The commercial action of 'buy–sell' is fundamentally contingent on economic and market forces. While the two time characteristics, efficiency and business cycle, are best managed through time–space considerations – discussed earlier – the time characteristic, *experience*, which is embedded within the business cycle, is best managed via the time-action dimension. Experiences (or events and occurrences) and the quality of experiences deeply influence the buy-sell transaction.

Economic transaction concludes when a consumer buys a product or a service from the producer. However, the buy–sell transaction itself gets prompted through several actors and market mechanisms. The time–action dimension helps to evaluate this relationship between the producer and the consumer based on supply or demand side of economics, and a third phenomenon gaining momentum, the community enabled attitudinal economics. The supply side and demand side economics, broadly determines price vis-à-vis the economies of scale while the attitudinal economics determines prices based on community collectiveness or by provoking outrageous thinking like making today's scarce resources abundantly available in the future.

The classical manufacturer or the supplier of goods and services (also called 'pipeline businesses' by Parker, Van Alstyne and Choudary in their book *Platform Revolution*) drives from the supply side of the business with a primary objective of reducing cost across the supply chain thereby increasing profit. During market contraction, money supply reduces and so does customer demand, and hence the net impact is lowered production and huge pressure on margins. For a pipeline business the normal response would be cost cutting – first by reducing any waste and then by reducing variable capacity costs in line with reduction in capacity.

The classical buyer on the other side represents the demand side of the equation. A buyer is willing to buy a good or a service at a specific price that normally denotes the price-to-value ratio that he is willing to pay for at that point in time. As the price increases, the desire to buy reduces, and vice-versa. Thus, the equilibrium between the supply side and the demand side is a price discovery that satisfies both the buyer and the seller and is the market equilibrium. In short, the supply side is spurred via lowered costs and innovation, while the demand side is spurred by improving buying power or via discounts.

The supply side and the demand side have always been the two sides of the market equilibrium equation, corresponding to the providers and buyers – the creators of goods and services, versus, the consumers of goods and services. The entire supply chain including the intermediaries has so far been directly or indirectly owned by the manufacturers and providers – displaying supply side economics. With the advent of electronic platforms (Amazon, Uber, Airbnb), a new intermediary that primarily represents the buyers and aggregates their demand has surfaced, which Parker, Alstyne and Choudary refer, to as "Platform Revolution." A platform is successful only if buyers transact; hence it is imperative for the platform owners to induce buying activity. This means that a platform also needs subscription from a lot of goods and services providers – the wider the choice of providers, the more likely that a buy–sell transaction gets consummated on the platform. Thus, the creation of large-scale corporations, possible earlier only via the supply side economics and at a very tedious speed, was now possible at a significant faster rate by leveraging the buy-side economics and platforms and the valuable networks resulting from it. Hence the business model too, was a derivative of the 'network effect.'

This also supports the efficient market mechanism. Since there are a large number of suppliers on the platform, a much wider choice of product specifications that satisfies the need of a specific buyer is more likely. Thus, a transaction is likely to conclude at a fair and optimum price. However, for the platform owners, the cost of customer acquisition as well as of the frequent discounting keeps their profit weak till they reach a threshold. The law of supernormal profit dictates that whenever there is abnormal profit, more players jump in thereby increasing the supply and consequently reducing the profits; this is also true for the platforms. So far, many platforms despite having weak financials have survived on valuations and dilution of their stock or cross-subsidy, while the platforms are themselves competing on rules dictated by the supply side. Amazon has competition from Alibaba and Flipkart (now Walmart), Uber from Ola and Airbnb from Oyo. The supply side impact has begun, and the platforms are in desperate search of lowered costs and higher profits – a supply side compulsion, by curating products and services that can potentially deliver higher value to the customers and profits to the platforms.

Economics has only two known sides – the supply side and the demand side, and the price elasticity is a critical lever for both to adjust their product pricing and the consequent volume of sales. However, the boundary conditions do present an interesting third alternative as it helps transcend the innate human behavior from a pure economic consideration to a spirit of defiant ambition and undiluted hope, and sometimes, even bordering on contemptuous arrogance. This is yet another powerful extension seen rapidly expanding into another form of producer-consumer relationship – *The Attitudinal Economics.*

At extreme boundary conditions, the price elasticity theoretically means that at zero price there should be infinite buyers, and likewise, at an infinite price (read: very high) there should be zero buyers. But is this premise consistently true at these endpoints? The two examples that follow prove otherwise.

Chef Hemant Oberoi's tryst with The Zodiac Grill at Taj Mahal Hotel in Mumbai, in the opening story, is living proof that price elasticity at the first endpoint is not necessarily always true; 'pay-what-you-want' can be an equally rewarding business strategy when used in appropriate situations.

In one of his interviews, Hemant recalls that on its inaugural day patrons paid as high as Rupees 3000 per head (then equivalent to USD 200) for the meal. Nearly nobody underpaid. The restaurant continued to run in this format for some time before it turned itself into a firmly priced menu a few years later. On its 25th anniversary, a few years ago, it ran a 25-course dinner priced at USD 500 apiece – not a price that one would often see in India even today.

Many such experiments have been successfully run around the world in recent times, more in the restaurant world, but many others for theater shows, musical performances, a band selling their music and even a football club offering its match tickets. In general, businesses have not lost money. Although there have always been a few customers who have not paid anything, most have paid what they thought was fair, and some paid much more than the fair value, reported the BBC, while covering the 'pay-as-you-want' format across a variety of events. So how does this seemingly breach of an economic law work in real life? The answer lies in trust and an implicit accountability towards the community or what can be loosely termed as 'attitudinal' economics. As long as the customer experiences something new, he will keep coming back to pay more, but as the novelty wears off, he is likely to pay less. This is a mechanism that organizations use to introduce customers to their products without the customers feeling the risk of being first-time users. It is also used effectively to deploy the nudge theory – a small amount being charged with the main bill for charity, or just as a price discovery tool.

Dating back to sometime in 1991, the Open Source movement was 'accidentally' triggered by Linus Torvalds when he decided to publish his version of the UNIX kernel to the software community at large. The Linux operating system was thus born. His main aim was not altruistic but was to request for comments on his code. The community, hungry for access to code whose usage was neither commercially licensed nor disallowed for modification, soon started to publish new features, feature extensions and even defect fixes for the existing code. Thus, open source was born. Over time Linux not only became the main UNIX version for nearly all computing machine manufacturers but was also the seed for Android. Further, in 2005, Linus wrote a fully distributed source code control system, GIT, which has recently been bought by Microsoft, strangely, the fiercest adversary of LINUX, thus indicating a huge shift in thinking of large software houses towards open source. Today a very minuscule percentage of the overall LINUX code is Linus', but the feature-rich software is thriving because of thousands of global contributors. The reasons for the contributions remain selfish and combative, although not necessarily commercial.

The attitudinal economics is akin to a movement that invokes a common cause via a collective action to strengthen the weak or via a combative action to weaken the giants in their own bastions. Another example is the attempt to make scarce resources abundantly available in the future

– be it space travel, space colonialization, autonomous cars
or energy supply, something that Elon Musk has volunteered
to deliver. His approach is to extend the platform rules of
reuse and waste, discussed later, to attitudinal economics and
harness the same to reduce cost to such outrageous levels
such that it comes within the reach of the common man. In
India, Reliance-Jio Telecom has offered unlimited free voice
calls for lifetime and now has added free bandwidth too. In a
segment that is struggling to make reasonable profits, Jio makes
significantly higher profits than its peers and is adored by the
stock market.

The 2 × 2 table (Table 3.1) encapsulates the time–action
discussion. However, each one of the three economic
forces, the supply side, the demand side and the attitudinal
businesses, view the core business elements and the associated
fundamentals very differently. The key differences are listed
below. Some of these differences between the demand and the
supply side were highlighted by Parker et al. referenced earlier.

Economic interactions: For pipeline businesses, the
producer–consumer interactions are customer-need based;

Table 3.1 The Producer–Consumer Relationships

		Consumers	
		Buyer or end user	*Community driven/ community believed co-curators*
Producers	*Curator (may own IP)*	Platform	Open source
	Owns IP	Pipeline	Pay-as-you-want or commoditized

consumers are either brand loyal or depend upon friends and acquaintances or research to make such decisions. For platform business, it is the wide variety of options available that scores on the purchase decision; consumers form a community on the platform and depend upon user reviews to make purchase decisions. For attitudinal economics, a common purpose or a faraway dream can be the catalyst to invoke such a transaction; it now transcends from just community to community and crowd.

Assets: A key mindset that differentiates the pipeline and platform businesses is their approach to capex. 'Revenues minus expenses equals profits' and businesses must generate profits for its shareholders is an undisputable truth. The question is how much time the shareholders are willing to give before they become impatient. The profits are needed partly to plow back into business to fuel further growth and partly to be distributed to the shareholders. Shareholders earn profits also by selling their stockholdings when the stock prices of the firm go above their purchase costs. Since stock prices reflect future earnings of a firm, despite continuous losses, a stock could trade above its book value basis the holding horizon (read patience) of the investor who is willing to pay the price multiples. When the shares are not listed, the valuation is determined by the PE (Private Equities), and provided all other parameters – revenues, number of customers, reach, etc. – are showing an upward trend, valuation can be deemed to be increasing over time. Since all these metrics are based on quality and quantity of customers, the customer acquisition and retention are also the places where the money is spent. While pipeline business spend capital on building physical infrastructure, platforms spend money on technology and platforms to improve the ease of transaction and deducing customer behavior insights. Successful platform businesses like Amazon and Uber have also started to invest in physical and owned infrastructure to reduce costs, improve customer experience and hence increase stickiness.

In instances of attitudinal economics, the initial asset is nearly always created by the producer. However, the consumption and the pricing are based on the implicit assumption that most people are fair and at least some are willing to experiment with something unique. This creates a community and over time surfaces common vision and trust within the community ecosystem. When the community ceases to see something that is of value or that aligns to their vision the novelty and the association wear off and the experiment dies. When the community sees continuously evolving value but restricted by the inability of the producer to put in unending resources, they pitch in by mobilizing resources through crowd sourcing or putting in their personal efforts. The greater the size of the community, the lower the chances of such an engagement failing, as evident from the success of the open source movement.

Yet another dimension of the attitudinal economics is on making what is scarce and hence highly priced, into abundant and widely available. They are not only in software but also hardware, computing power, energy, education, healthcare, voice, bandwidth, future space travel, etc., and the list goes on. The mechanism is to make the ordinary person taste the exquisite, the out-of-reach or a wide range of options without any ownership but in small modicums either via the subscription model, the pay-as-you-use model or pay-what-you-want models. But, of course, there will always be the segment of customers who will like to be the owners of the unique.

Scale: Pipeline businesses are firmly established on supply economies of scale. Platform businesses are predicated on demand economies of scale. The open source or pay-as-you-want businesses are based on attitudinal economies or community collaboration of scale. The variants are crowd-sourcing and crowd-funding. The community collaboration is very different from the economic collaboration. The former relies on enormous power from the mass-movement while the latter, between two equals.

Resource wastage and leveraging unutilized resource: Pipeline businesses' view of wastage is restricted to the supply chain being operated and controlled by them, but a platform business views any resource, unutilized or partly utilized or that can be co-utilized, as its asset base. For example, an empty bedroom in a house, empty passenger seat(s) when a car user is driving his car, or an existing consumer base of an FMCG being sold only single class of goods, is viewed as waste. It is a greener, more optimal and potentially socialistic view of running a business in a capitalistic world and at the same time closely aligning to one of the most prolific capitalists, Jack Welsh's, view of "your assets must sweat." Even rockets are reusable now.

The ecommerce fraternity in India has pushed such an economy of scope to a limit far beyond what Uber or Airbnb have been able to achieve. Delivery of milk every morning to households by delivery boys is common practice even today in India, as it is in the west for delivery of morning newspapers. Online grocery stores are now utilizing these delivery boys to deliver morning groceries to the same households at a fraction of a cost they would have incurred in running their own delivery trucks. This is improving the earnings of the bicycle riding milk delivery boys, as well as keeping logistics and delivery costs low for the ecommerce and online-based grocery stores too.

In attitudinal economics, companies force-collaborate with each other to avoid the re-creation of yet another similar product for the sake of competing with a rival firm – this is especially true now in the software industry. This takes avoidance of wastage to a new level. Organizations, especially in technology, are joining hands to fund products that help to improve portability, interoperability and reuse and some of the best examples are the service mesh – istio, the blockchain Hyperledger Fabric or the micro services architecture. The software industry has been the cause for rapid disruption in every industry, including its own, due to digital adoption being such a natural consequence of attitudinal economies of scale. This will only increase in future.

Product variants: Pipeline business package customer preferences and needs as characteristics in the variants of the products that they sell; such variants are usually few. Hence the products are designed on generic and broader market requirements with a few sub-categories. On the other hand, in a platform business, since there is just an aggregation of demand duly matched to a group of suppliers supplying similar products but with very specific characteristic differences, the chances of getting a more accurate fit between the buyer and the seller becomes enormous. This also means that the number of product sub-categories available are much higher. Hence the bigger the subscriber base, the better are the chances of a lower cost and a higher fit.

In attitudinal economics instances like open source, since communities share the process of creation, they also take active part in creating the roadmap. Each community member has access to the code and can add extensions to suit his specific needs. This, in turn, when shared with the community, makes the application richer, broader and deeper. This is a selfishly virtuous cycle that makes it infinitely sustainable.

The *time–action* dimension is the most powerful tool for a firm to align its strategic actions to scale based on the levers of supply side, demand side or attitudinal economics. The time dimension corresponds to contraction, steady and growth strategies while the action dimension corresponds to optimize, preserve and expand strategies.

Based on the time–action demarcations the most potent strategies that can be adopted are along *contraction–optimize*, *steady–preserve* and *growth–expand* sub-segments. Since there are just three basic actions – create/add, change/preserve and destroy/simplify, all the dictates of supply-side economics are fully applicable to the contraction–optimize sub-segment.

Whether the going is tough or not, continuous weeding out of waste and improvement in productivity, quality and engagement scores is mandatory just to survive and offset operating expense inflation. A continuous green metric over a large period of time should flag a potential red as there lies inadvertently hidden capacity and waste. The supply-side economics dictates fit in well here.

The *steady–preserve* sub-segment signifies growth. Both the top line as well as the bottom line should show an upward trajectory. To preserve the lead, which a firm enjoys in the market, continuous experimentation, innovation and value injection is needed. This is also the sub-segment of continuous evolution and change. Cannibalizing existing products to create new ones (e.g., Apple), or continuously improving customer experience (e.g., Amazon), is a frequent strategy for the highly successful firms. Provoking demand is equally critical – either the markets are buoyant, or there is increased buying demand and discretionary spends. This is the time when firms are willing to take investment risks and incentivize buyer behavior including discounting to spur buying. This is also the point where traditional pipe companies resort to the lure of the platform and get on to it – like Nike or even GE and Bosch, as they adapt themselves to operating in the areas of wellness, industrial Internet and autonomous life. Jack Ma launched the 'world singles day' sale on Alibaba in 2009. He sold one billion USD worth of goods on Alibaba in the first hour. The 2019 edition clocked sales of one billion USD in the first 68 seconds and sold 12 billion USD in the first hour! The total sales generated in the day was 38.4 billion USD, the largest ever on any ecommerce platform, globally. In the *steady–preserve* sub-segment, both the supply and demand side economic approaches can thrive although the demand side will always have an edge.

The *growth–expand* sub-segment defines hope, change, speed and disruption. There are no previous benchmarks and the achievement seems dreamlike, the scale, shocking. The attitudinal economics is geared to make today's shortages as surpluses. It holds no boundaries in taking an outrageous idea and delivering it. Musk is one such example. Without having defense, automotive or energy industry expertise he has challenged what was the domain of two of the most powerful nations of the world embedded deeply into space, or the world's most powerful automotive lobby or the large energy giants. He broke the assumption that space rockets were not reusable, or cars cannot be completely autonomous, or energy supply not be in abundance. While his first business is grounded on platform rules, and the other two are on attitudinal rules, it is a matter of time when all three could exhibit attitudinal characteristics. It will also be a matter of fact that robots will write code and software will become free between communities and robotic ecosystems. The supply, demand and attitudinal economics, all fit in here, although it is the mindset of the last that stands the best chance to explode.

3.5 In Summary

- The interplay of areas bounded by two axes at a time give rise to three powerful tools for strategic planning – time and space, space and action, and, time and action.
- Since time embodies opportunities; space symbolizes resistance and hence, strength; and action exemplifies force and thus activity:
  - **Time–space** dimension helps align a firm its strength to opportunities.
  - **Space–action** dimension helps build strong competitive advantage via market-engagement actions.
  - **Time–action** dimension helps in evaluating the producer–consumer relationships to adopt supply-side, demand-side or attitudinal economics. While the

elements of time are embedded in the business cycle, the buy–sell action is predicated on economic and market forces.

- **Time–space** has three sub-segments:
  - **Contraction–own:** Exploit opportunities best suited to *own–strengths* for driving business of today; however, both strengths and opportunities can be mistakenly over exaggerated.
  - **Steady–known:** Explore opportunities by extending strengths – *leveraged and supplementary* – to known spaces for business of tomorrow; cross selling, acquisitions and alliances are deployed.
  - **Growth–unknown:** Unearth explosive opportunities from long-term threats as *disruptive strengths* as businesses of the future; firms must allocate 'budget for failure' to tread on this path.
  - Companies cannot remain indefinitely in contraction–own state; based on the *law of scaling*, firms show sub-linear scaling with growth, displaying economies of scale; they also have a finite lifespan at the same time – thus they need to continuously reinvent and transform themselves.
- **Space–action** has three sub-segments
  - **Own–optimize:** Improving the price-value equation continuously by re-engineering, innovating and optimizing to give more at lower costs; incremental innovation and operational improvements with direct go-to-market. *Surviving the market.*
  - **Known–preserve:** Innovating new products and expand into adjacent market; leveraged differentiation, strategic innovation sustaining go-to-market. *Thriving the market.*
  - **Unknown–expand:** Breakthrough innovation and disruptive go-to-market; usually transformative in nature. *Driving the market.*
- **Time–action:**

- Economic transaction concludes when a consumer buys a product or a service from the producer at a price agreeable to both.
- Pipeline business drives from supply side with the primary objective of driving down costs and increasing profits.
- Platforms are aggregators of demand; hence drives business from demand side economics.
- At extreme boundary conditions of price elasticity – infinite price should have zero buyers and at zero price there would be infinite buyers; however, the premise is not always true. Pay-what-you-want format does make money; this is an example of attitudinal economics.
- Attitudinal economics is akin to a movement that invokes a common cause via a collective effort to weaken giants in their own territory (open source or pay-as-you-want) or make scarce resources available abundantly in future (space travel, property on Mars).
- The three differ in their approach towards ownership, assets, scale, wastage, leverage and product variants.
- **Contraction–Optimize:** Subscribes to the mechanics of supply-side economics.
- **Steady–Preserve:** Supports both options of supply and demand side economics.
- **Growth–Expand:** Is applicable to all – supply-side, demand-side and attitudinal economics.

Selected Bibliography – Section I

Applegate, Lynda M. and Harreld, Bruce. 2009,*Don't Just Survive—Thrive: Leading Innovation in Good Times and Bad*, Working Paper 09–127, Harvard Business School.

BEA, July 2012, Final Report – On the accident on June 1, 2009 to the Airbus A330–203 registered F-GZCP operated by Air France flight AF 447 Rio de Janeiro – Paris, Bureau d'Enquêtes et d'Analyses. www.bea.aero/docspa/2009/f-cp090601.en/pdf/f-cp090601.en.pdf

Brown, Harvey R. and Lehmkuhl, Dennis. 2013, *Einstein, the Reality of Space, and the Action–Reaction Principle*, Cornell University Library. arXiv: History and Philosophy of Physics

Bryson, Bill. 14 September 2004, *A Short History of Nearly Everything*, Broadway Books, Reprint edition.

Clausewitz, Carl von. 1873, *On War*, English Translation.

Clavell, James. 1983, *The Art of War, Sun Tsu*, Edited by James Clavell, Delacorte Press.

Dalal, Phorom. November 16, 2014, Chef Hemant Oberoi gets nostalgic as Zodiac Grill turns 25, Midday, Mumbai www.mid-day.com/articles/chef-hemant-oberoi-gets-nostalgic-as-zodiac-grill-turns-25/15768194

Davenport, Thomas H. and Patil, D.J. October 2012, Data scientist: The sexiest job of the 21st century, *Harvard Business Review.*

Gulati, Ranjay, Nohria, Nitin, and Wohlgezogen, Franz. March 2010, Roaring out of recession, *Harvard Business Review.*

Leatherdale, Duncan. July 22, 2015, Do pay-what-you-want pricing strategies really work? BBC News. www.bbc.com/news/uk-england-33609867

Mankani, Sneha, November 2014, 25 course-menu feed your appetite opulence, *Vogue.* www.vogue.in/content/25-course-menu-feed-your-appetite-opulence/#pan-seared-pomfret-with-asparagus-spears-at-the-zodiac-grill

News Release. May 19, 2016, Life expectancy increased by 5 years since 2000 but health inequalities persist by World Health Organization, Geneva. www.who.int/en/news-room/detail/19-05-2016-life-expectancy-increased-by-5-years-since-2000-but-health-inequalities-persist

Nobel Prize citation for Physiology/ Medicine 2017 to Jeffrey C. Hall, Michael Rosbash and Michael W. Young, for their discoveries of molecular mechanisms controlling the circadian rhythm, 2017, Why is the circadian clock important? www.nobelprize.org/prizes/medicine/2017/summary/

Parker Geoffrey G., Van Alstyne, Marshall W., and Choudary, Sangeet Paul. 2016, *Platform Revolution*, W. W. Norton & Co.

Pentland, Alex. 2015, *Social Physics – How Social Networks Can Make Us Smarter*, Penguin Books.

Ross, Nick and Tweedie, Neil. April 28, 2012, Damn it! We're going to crash! *The Telegraph*, UK. www.telegraph.co.uk/technology/9231855/Air-France-Flight-447-Damn-it-were-going-to-crash.html

Spencer, Herbert. 1867, *First Principles by Williams and Norgate*, London, Second edition.

Thapar, Romila. 2002, *The Penguin History of Early India – From the Origins to AD1300*, Penguin Books, India.

Vasconcellos, Dr Jorge. 2003, *Strategy Moves*, Financial Times/Prentice Hall.

West, Geoffrey. 2017, *The Universal Laws of Growth, Innovation and Scale – Sustainability in Organisms, Economies, Cities and Companies*, Wiedenfeld & Nicolson,

Wise, Jeff. December 6, 2011, What really happened aboard air France 447? Popular Mechanics www.popularmechanics.com/flight/a3115/what-really-happened-aboard-air-france-447-6611877/

Strategy Triangles

Driving Successful Outcomes

"No rhythm without repetition in time and space, without reprises, without returns... [but] there is always something new and unforeseen that introduces itself into the repetitive: difference."

– Henri Lefebvre

Chapter 4

Driving Business in Multiple Frames of Decision-Making

In a three-dimensional world, we have no control over time. However, we do have control over the choice of space and the timing of execution of actions within that space. Thus, decision-making boils down to choosing a combination of space and action levers based on the prevailing operating environment or 'time-conditions', such that the combination has the maximum likelihood of delivering the planned objectives successfully. Decision-making can be either centralized, de-centralized or collaborative, and once made, is followed by an action plan. Every action is time constrained and the elapsed time between the decision-making and the execution of the actions, or the urgency, is dependent upon the state of the environment, whether stable or volatile, and the criticality of the objective.

When plans go awry, subsequent decision-making and reaction speeds for further responses become even more important. It is the state of the environment and the operating space that determines whether the ensuing decision-making and control would continue to remain centralized or get implicitly passed over to the team on the ground. To explain this further, following is a table (Table 4.1) that depicts the relationship between the state of environment (the time axis) and the operating space (the space axis) and its impact on the dynamics of continuous decision-making within the teams.

'Volatile' environment is one that is marked by rapid changes and the teams either do not have enough resources to control the state or do not have enough time to elaborately plan and respond to these changes. The more volatile the environment, the greater is the need for rapid-action response. 'Stable' environments, on the other hand, are those where changes are gradual, and teams have either enough resources at hand or enough time to respond.

The need for complete *alignment with key objectives* is especially pronounced when teams are operating in *highly volatile environments and unknown spaces*, where it is not always feasible to consult before taking decisions. This is critical, for example, in a covert operation (while flushing

Table 4.1 Basis for Engagement and Continuous Decision-Making within Teams during Volatile and Stable Environments

		Business Environment	
		Volatile	*Stable*
Space	*Unknown*	Basis: Overall key objectives and trust in judgement Decision-making: Real time and on ground	Basis: Learning and feedback Decision-making: Collaborative and alignment
	Own	Basis: Specific sub-objective Decision-making: Command and control	Basis: Establishment of operational control limits on the output metrics Decision-making: Manage by exception

out terrorists holed inside a blacked-out hotel building that is full of resident guests, or, when on a group trek in an unchartered terrain a part of the group gets separated). The teams are usually well briefed on the overall objectives of the operation and regardless of the absence or availability of the command-and-control chains, they are expected to take decisions that help in traversing in the direction of those objectives. The same is true in volatile business contexts, like stock-trading desks or during customer negotiations where similar fundamentals of decision-making are expected. However, boundary conditions need to be well laid out to avoid rogue, runaway outcomes like the demise of the 225-year-old Barings Bank, overnight.

In *volatile environments but within own spaces*, the decision-making and engagement with the teams is the absolute opposite – command-and-control. The space is fully understood and needs defense from an impending outage. Take for example, advancing cyclones and other natural disasters where pre-evacuation and disaster relief needs to be managed – very specific instructions are given and enforced. Where the power to enforce does not exist, strong advisories are given. Similarly, in business environments, when a substantially ailing organization has top management changes, continuous command and control is deployed. Every sub-objective (e.g., cost control, consolidation, time bound import substitution, etc.) is run as a separate program and continuously measured. This is the general story of a typical turnaround.

When the environment is stable and outcomes predictable, the decision-making and team engagement becomes more decentralized. In such situations, continuous and corrective instructions on sustained basis would be rare and more likely be metrics driven, which reverses only when outcomes are beyond the agreed control limits. Thus, in *stable environments within known and owned spaces*, 'management by exception,' is the usual norm. This suggests that the operations are mature, and the limits of deviation have already been established. When outcomes begin to move out of such control limits repeatedly, only then does a substantive intervention becomes necessary. This corresponds to managing production lines or sales pipelines, which are the day-to-day imperatives of a business.

Likewise, in *stable environments but unknown spaces*, e.g., expansion into new territories, acquisition of delivery organization in a foreign country, operating a new foreign subsidiary, or, acquisition of a firm in an area where the acquiring company doesn't have strength but is extending its capability through the acquired company, the 'learn and align' engagement model is largely adopted. In such situations, both the *alignment of key objectives across the organization and close monitoring of outcomes* becomes necessary for achieving success. Subsequent decision-making is based on continuous feedback, learning and collaboration between the central and the arms.

Every organization has immediate-term, mid-term and long-term objectives and these three usually run in parallel, though at some point, some fuse into each other seamlessly while a few get deprioritized and dropped and new ones join the list. The leadership needs to continually evaluate strategies based on rapidly changing business cycles, market conditions, competition changers and other external stimuli to keep all the objectives current and in line with goals and mission. Usually macro factors, largely outside an enterprise's control, are causes of such sudden strategy adjustments. The second factor is largely around relentless competition and technology disruptions that influence such changes. Competition changers are those inflection points in time when the fight moves from 'battling for today' to 'competing for the future.' Of course, internal reasons like hidden skeletons, poor cash flows, customer attrition, runaway projects, lawsuits, etc., can too alter the course of an enterprise, but these are operational matters that a competent leadership is expected to manage.

For a listed company, the single composite measure that identifies a respected organization (may not always be well run though) is the stock price and the direction in which the price has been trending vis-à-vis the industry average or its immediate competitors. A company is rewarded with an increasing stock-price when it is seen to be adding value consistently to its employees, customers and the shareholders. Thus, the core objectives must include a specific value generation agenda towards all the three stakeholders on a constant basis. Sometimes such programs are run across multiple years or even in perpetuity.

In running business operations, there are six key areas that need to be closely managed – revenues, profits, growth from existing customers, acquisition of new customers, people engagement and, lastly, production (all inclusive) and innovation. These are achieved through the firm's strategic business plan and its products and services catalogue. The strategic business plan is a standard document that an organization lives by. These are business goals and the initiatives through which the goals are planned to be met. Usual *strategic business planning cycle* consists of a three or a five-year overall objective, based on which yearly business plans are created, reviewed and adjusted. Every product or service that is marketed and sold to customers traverses through its own *product lifecycle* viz. through development and introduction, growth, maturity and, then, demise. Firms needs to continuously identify reasonably opportune points in time to cannibalize their existing products and re-launch upgraded and advanced versions, or, withdraw the product at its end-of-life – a place where it makes no economic sense to sustain it. Finally, the external *business/market cycle* superimposes how easy or difficult achieving this would be. The interplay of these three critical cycles that a firm must continuously monitor and adjust to, is represented and managed on the three fundamental axes.

The strategic business plan describes actions vis-à-vis own objectives and is representable on the action axis. The business and market cycle are the general market conditions within which a business operates and oscillates over time and is represented on the time axis. The product and services lifecycle are largely affected by innovation in the market and a product can quickly go out of fashion due to competitive response – hence, it is represented on the space axis.

4.1 Time–Space Planning – Across Multiple Horizons

This section begins by glossing over some of the known obvious. For any firm the equation, revenue minus expenses equals profits, is a central theme to its continued existence; how this equation can be maximized in the short and the long terms, forms a critical part of the business planning and its subsequent execution. No organization wants to run with a negative equation, at least for long, and although revenues and profits are critical, cash generation and positive cash flows are equally crucial parameters for sustained growth. Thus, for most firms, planning for efficient operations that is likely to generate profits and cash from its core business, and at the same time prioritizing investments into products, capacity and markets in the near to medium term, is a key goal; sustained growth via organic (and inorganic) means in the longer term, is next. Equally critical is planning for contingencies and emergencies as the business environment, markets, and the operating uncertainties, can severely impact normal running of the business.

Planning can broadly be of four types – *strategic, tactical, operational and emergent–transactional*, corresponding to the long-term, medium-term, near-term and immediate-term respectively. These four can also be viewed as planning much-ahead-of-time, ahead-of-time, just-in-time and behind-time. Though the genesis of these four planning types is from the theatre of war, the term, 'emergent or transactional,' has been used to signify corrective and contingent responses needed to combat aberrant occurrences. There is yet one other important intermediate state that we often merge or miss – 'operationalization,' which lies between the tactics and operations and represents the phase of commissioning and readiness before the steady operations begin. Any initial setup and pilot runs are deemed to be part of the operationalization process.

Although humans and organizations are both living beings, their genetic makeup and survival response mechanisms are very different. Most humans are torn between the anguish of the past and the fear of the future, while mostly ignoring the present. On the contrary, most organizations bask in the glory of past and assume that the present and the future are likely to be guaranteed on similar terms; what gave them success in the past would continue to do so in future too. Both positions are incorrect. The past is a great teacher of learning and of experience, while the future is a dream that needs to be shaped. It needs to be carefully crafted and brought to fruition through a judicious use of present.

Human beings are interminably consumed between fulfilling 'needs' and generating 'wants.' We perceive needs to be immediate and make fulfilling of those needs a very high priority in our lives. Most needs revolve around the basic and urgent necessities of life that includes food, clothing, shelter, medicines and education. 'Wants,' on the other hand, are good-to-haves; these are societal symbols that signify goals and aspirations which are potentially achievable, but with significant amount of effort or struggle. 'Wants' thus represent a future state. As we grow in society and in stature, 'wants' become more pronounced and mutate into 'needs.' Most choices emanate from the impact on today versus the impact on tomorrow. For most of us, liquidating bills in the immediate term, planning for holidays or a new car in the medium term and budgeting for a new house or higher education of children in the longer term is usual.

Any *strategy* is fueled by 'wants' and is the overall objective of a "campaign" or a "plan" that is expected to achieve an intended outcome. Strategy emanates from the goals, purposes and objectives of an organization or an individual; it generally sets the long-term direction. Strategy involves choices based on information, usually associated with insights and understanding of future trends and discontinuities. When the insights are privileged, or the understanding of the trends inspired, the impact can be truly transformational. Strategy thus impacts the future more than today. Strategy is also synonymous with differentiation or source of advantage (to incapacitate competition), although sustained differentiation is quietly becoming a slippery edge. The key to successful differentiation is in the difference that delivers better value to customers, whether it is in the price, the processes, the intellectual property or a competitive advantage an organization has. A strategy need not necessarily always be to deliver a long-term goal, especially when deployed in highly volatile environments. An effective strategy for volatile environments could be in achieving a series of short or medium-term goals, refining inputs at each step and being prepared for better responses to highly fluctuating stimuli. Such conditions determine if the firm needs to adopt a one-year, a three-year or a five-year strategy. Strategy thus is the agreed course of path that an organization has decided to pursue to achieve its intended long-term objectives. Strategy is well thought out and documented, is slow and difficult to reverse, allows for deliberations and evaluation of alternatives, and needs a much larger strength of will to take difficult decisions.

Fulfilling 'needs' is immediate and urgent and thus warrants no or little strategy. A sick child needs medical attention – whether the parents have the money or not. Any helplessness in times of 'needs' accentuates irrationality and evokes the abnormal, and sometimes even dangerous behavior. Needs may be real or perceived and even perceived needs can generate responses like real needs. Many wars have been fought for egocentric needs of punishing perceived wrong doing. Many business decisions, like building a hospital for the poor, have been based on the need to eradicate the self-suffered feeling of helplessness from others.

Tactics defines the specifics of the engagement and details the steps, including any fine tuning, that may be needed to achieve the overall strategy. A single business transaction cannot determine the final net gain; however, it is important that any success is followed through by a force multiplier. Therefore, in the mind, one should have already planned a series of moves with likely permutations of their outcomes. Thus, executing strategy comprises many sequential complete acts called *tactics* that are dependent on detailed steps and 'tactical' planning. Tactics helps in adjustments on ground for fine tuning the strategy, as plans usually don't endure for long without warranting modification. There should have, however, been enough diligence done in evaluating all risks with alternate tactics ready to be deployed when necessary. Often, unplanned conditions occur, and ad-hoc tactics need to be employed to perform course correction.

Business *operations* signifies repetitiveness in providing sustained delivery of products and services to customers. Operations corresponds to a set of repetitive procedures to generate a specific output and achieve the tactic repeatedly. It is the combination of tasks, processes and actions performed by the functional and support organizations to deliver a product or service of value to customers. The prime objective is to use the assets to maximize production, deliver high quality, control cost of delivery, improve efficiency, reduce defects and inject large measures of innovation on a continual basis. Operations are governed by business metrics and financial outcomes, generally comparable to competitors of similar size (in some cases different sizes too), within the same industry and specifically based on the organization's vision. Often benchmarks are run across industries to create best in class metrics. Industry best practices are embedded into the management systems of an organization enabling it with continual improvement. Usually operations are managed by exceptions, closely monitored between the upper and lower control limits of relevant metrics and statistics.

Operationalization is a critical step that lies between the tactics and the operations but is often forgotten or informally executed. The more complex the operations, the more critical is the *operationalization* – a term that too has been borrowed from the lexicon of war. For a battle offensive to be successful, troops, armaments, decoys and battle-supporting functions like medical supplies, doctors, food supplies, air cover, etc., need to be moved into their position before the actual battle begins. The entire logistical planning and the pre-positioning of the above is the operationalization phase of a battle. Likewise, for business operations to be successful, people, machinery, money and other supporting functions and processes, like quality, HR, facilities, procurement, etc., need to be in position before full-fledged operations can be commenced. The procurement and setting up of the machines in a factory, testing it to run and producing a trial batch that is within the required quality and operational parameters, form part of the operationalization phase. This is an extremely critical phase as the sign-off here signifies that the firm is ready to go live with its operations. Sometimes market conditions or resource crunch do not allow enough time to operationalize and warrant immediate action. Such cases, in Ray Bradbury's words, are like "jumping off the cliff and building your wings on the way down." Even if the unknowns are very high it is best to start the counteroffensive immediately than to wait for measured inputs and response.

Emergent transactions are like an emergency response team's action. They are corrective responses, meant to stem rapidly any deviations from expected outcomes. It is

especially the case when the combination of Murphy's Law
(i.e., something went wrong or unplanned at an inappropriate
time), coupled with deterioration due to wear and tear, have
struck in tandem, because the degradation had been gradual
and missed from being detected or arrested. Anything can
go wrong – plans can go awry, and operations, haywire.
Organizations usually adopt the likes of six-sigma to keep
such occurrences under check. However, it is not the
identified or the controllable variables but the uncontrollable
variables that cause the most grinding halts. Such disruptive
behavior that causes deviations from the expected result has
been termed 'emergent transactions.' Whenever a disruptive
transaction occurs, remedial steps need to be taken to course
correct – regardless of it being the strategy, tactic or the
operation that has gone off beam.

*

It is oft said that hardships are the greatest generators of
opportunities. Emergent transactions too have a similar power
– to help uncover step improvements and big innovation ideas.
Whether it is an operational failure or a strategy breakdown
an 'outage' is not just a 'sudden fire that has erupted and
needs to be doused quickly.' It also provides the opportunity
to evaluate the occurrence and its root-cause. A critical lens to
view a repeating outage is its rate of recurrence and successive
impact, whether minor, medium or major – indicating
retardation, deterioration or acceleration, respectively, towards
the final failure.

If it is the first time that an outage of minor impact has
occurred, a quick fix followed by a root-cause analysis is
fine. A repeat occurrence indicates deterioration; faster
recurrence, evidenced by the reducing 'Mean Time between
Failures' (MTBF) with a progressively harder impact
suggests acceleration towards failure. Usually poor planning,
inadequate resources, mistakes, ignoring critical warnings,

incorrect assumptions, lack of governance and sometimes plain 'brushing under the carpet' syndrome are invariably linked to such situations.

The 2 × 2 following table (Table 4.2) encapsulates the impact and an appropriate response matrix that is aimed at maximizing results.

How and where the responses can be applied, is a derivative of Table 4.2 and tabulated in Table 4.3.

Table 4.3 summarizes appropriate responses and actions related to emergent situations arising out of strategic, tactical and operational issues and their impact. For example, the first row in the table is related to emergent-transactional situations arising out of operational/tactical issues with medium impact – for example, a support call took more time than allocated as the newly appointed resolution engineer did not know where to find the solution. Such an emergent–transactional situation will have a medium impact on the overall operations and the fix can be immediately applied through training on knowledge portals where all such incident solutions are

Table 4.2 Emergent Transactions Response Matrix

		Business Impact	
		Minor Impact/ Retardation	*Major and Lasting Impact*
Planning Horizon	*Operational/ tactical*	Fix Fine-tune Recalibrate	Replace Redesign Pre-empt
	Strategic	Simplify Substitute Strengthen	Breakthrough Transform

Table 4.3 Emergent Transaction, Response and Action Matrix

Horizon	Impact	Response	Action
Operational/tactical	Medium impact	Fix	Training, knowledge portals, assign mentor
		Fine-tune	Machines, processes, controls for improved output
		Recalibrate	Process control limits, over time, for continuous improvement
	Major impact	Replace	Parts, capex-based equipment, people
		Substitute	Import, part breaking down
		Redesign	Process, automation, governance
		Pre-empt	Preventive maintenance and support, governance, cash flow
Strategic	Medium impact	Simplify	Automate, speed and ease of execution, organizational restructure
		Strengthen	Function, process, team
	Major impact	Breakthrough	Market, business model, customer preference, value
		Transform	Unlearn, breakdown of strategic assumptions

catalogued. The last entry in the table looks at potential resolution for a strategic emergent–transactional situation with a major impact – for example, oil prices dipping down to 35 USD per barrel. This needs a transformational approach where every strategic assumption needs to be reviewed and qualified again. The easiest, of course, is to cartelize and moderate output; but if hydrogen and solar are the future of power, and the oil-producing countries want similar profits as today, they will have to transform oil extraction, transportation, refining and distribution.

*

'Multiple horizons' within the time–space ambit symbolizes longevity and sustenance. It is about what that the leader has created and has left behind as a legacy. He is like a movie star adored by multiple generations, each in their own unique way. Legacy thus is highly sustainable and has a very long shelf life. J.N. Tata left his legacy in the Tata Empire built on trust and eternal values; so, did Thomas Elva Edison by leaving a legacy of scientific inventions and innovation in General Electric. And so did the Mahatma (Gandhi), Abraham Lincoln, Martin Luther King and many others; they will be remembered for the legacy they left behind.

To conclude, Table 4.4 sums up what a successful organization exhibits when actions across multiple horizons represents a well-integrated and successful deployment of strategy, tactics, operations and emergent-response plans. It is not only horizontally in the table but daisy-chained vertically too. The test of efficacy is simple – if a firm formulates a three-year strategic business plan wherein the first-year targets are fully met, the second-year targets are revised slightly downwards and in the third year, a new three-year plan is created, then the planning assumptions and the subsequent plans are based on shifting sands.

Table 4.4 Time–Space Planning Efficacy – Differentiating between Thriving and Ailing Firms

Business Characteristics Horizon of Planning	Thriving and Good	Negative and Losing
Strategic	• Growth and margins that beat the market • Differentiated offerings leveraging true source of advantage • Value pricing • Innovation and market insights	• Unstable Business Metrics • Too often faced by business hardships followed by change. • Not reading market • Takeover candidate
Tactical	• Optimized supply chain • Reasonably well managed risks • Low slack	• Poor early warning systems • Need additional resources and changes in plan repeatedly
Operational	• Managed by exception • Ops and delivery exception • Metrics driven	• Higher exceptions and outages • Shortages and shortfalls • Delays and poor customer satisfaction
Emergent – Transactional	• Happy employees and customers • Very low deviations. • Serious emergency action gives rise to innovation.	• Work–life imbalance • Continuous firefighting • Emergency action burns serious money

4.2 Space–Action Planning – Market Entry and the Art of Occupying Space

Markets are aggressive and business environments fierce and competitive. Businesses are very often compared to wars, and war-like situations are euphemistically used and commonly substituted in business situations – the reasons, obvious. The sole intent of war is to impose supremacy and incapacitate the enemy by force. The sole reason for a business enterprise is to be a market leader and incapacitate the competitors by creating potentially sustained differentiation. The spirit is the same, the results probably a little less bloody but arguably, equally devastating. However, brand wars could be as bitter and war-like, the difference being that they strike at sensibilities rather than gouging the guts.

Most war strategies find a place in business strategy and so do war tactics and tools. Use of intelligence to out-maneuver, hostile acquisitions to annex competition, use of innovation as a deterrent and direct brand attack to initiate conflict are commonplace. However, there are obvious differences too. Business warfare spurs economic growth and competition is usually good for consumers; unlike severe disagreement and desire to suppress in a war, the competitive spirit and desire to excel drives business. Moreover, every country has a watchdog that frames rules and guidelines for all economic activities to take place in a transparent and free-market environment.

Four distinct periods in history have been carefully selected as they resemble typical business strategies for market entry – as an *early mover*, during the *growth period*, during *maturity* and during the *declining phase* for a product or a service. For each period, the war strategy and the tactics were different and so were their approach, effect and outcomes; they witnessed both friendly and hostile activities to annex land masses.

The early civilizations of Egypt, Mesopotamia and the Indus valley prospered between 4000 BC and 2500 BC. The boundaries were very stable, and settlements were driven by the need for silt deposits for farming along rivers and waterways. Man, for the first time, had domesticated cattle and pottery was needed to store food and grains. Enormous discoveries marked this period that included the wheel, hutments and farming implements. This was also one of the prime reasons why very few wars were reported during this period. The same is true for businesses too. For *early movers*, the competitive resistance and hostility faced is very low and capturing the market share is the easiest. Some of the early eCommerce businesses that struggled initially but went on to become behemoths like Amazon and Facebook, represent this phase. These were *competition changers*!

The first great empires began to form and thrive in the periods between 350 BC and 250 BC. These empires were defined by "extensive territory, monumental architecture and imperial proclamation." For the first time, Alexander the Great set out to conquer large parts of the world to create the first imperial empire. Chandragupta Maurya, his contemporary, was busy annexing parts of what is now modern India and is credited largely as the first unifier of the Indian sub-continent. Roughly 50 years later, the Chinese territory was also being unified and brought under the rule of Chin Dynasty through aggression and conquests.

History shows that there were many similarities; each king studied under the tutelage of a renowned mentor who shaped their strategies and conquests – it was Aristotle who taught Alexander and the famous Kautilya who tutored the young king Chandragupta Maurya; although Chin was largely influenced by the teachings of Confucius, he was not directly taught by him. Aristotle and Kautilya copiously documented the crafts of statehood, administration and warfare in their books which were used as a guide by their disciples. However, one of the best-known war strategists,

Sun Tzu, who had authored *The Art of War*, was also their contemporary and his strategies were rigorously followed by the Chin Chinese emperor.

The key strategies adopted during the period of great empires hinged on territorial expansion through war, alliances and matrimony. They integrated the vanquished and achieved both – expansion of territory as well as army. They used the expanse of the empire to balance excess produce in one area with shortages in the others, thus spurring free cross-territorial trade. The Great Empires continued for 300 more years at the hands of their respective descendants and many new ones like the Roman Empire were born. This was also the period where a lot of new religions were born to fight against human sufferings and depravity. The period is quite analogous to the *'growth phase'* of a business cycle.

During the growth phase market entry, consumers are willing to experiment but product quality, close customer interaction, retention, listening to the market voices and hence building the brand are extremely critical for firms to succeed. Some of the large brands like the Ford, GE and the Tata's would be key examples in this phase. Companies need to watch out for getting trapped in *the circle of self-incumbency*, discussed in the last chapter of this section, as many competitors try to establish and grow within the same market spectrum.

The beginning of the thirteenth century saw one of the most brutal and savage, but an extremely successful campaign that created an empire stretching from the Caspian Sea to the Pacific rim, with an area which was four times that of Alexander's empire. This was the Mongol empire under the conquests of Genghis Khan; which by 1300 AD, under Genghis' descendants had extended across 28 million square kilometers or roughly one-fifth of the land mass of earth. Quite unlike the strategies of rulers of earlier periods, Genghis' actions emanated from his childhood experiences – poverty and humiliation. His troops looted, decimated and mass executed inhabitants of the vanquished towns leaving behind only dead and ruin. No one was spared – men, women or children. As the kingdom extended wide and large, Genghis ruled using fear and terror.

The business strategy for entry into a *mature market phase* is equally bloody as firms are storming into the bastions of their competitor. Undercutting price, large replacement discounts, competitor acquisition for the sole purpose of acquiring the customers and killing the competitor brand, etc. are typical strategies encountered. The fight between Amazon and Walmart-Flipkart, or, the US carmakers and the Japanese carmakers, or the fight for retaining standards, are some of the examples of this phase. Companies need to watch out for *encirclement by invaders*, more of which has been deliberated in Chapter 6.

The colonialization of large parts of the world by England, Portugal, Spain and France in the eighteenth and the nineteenth centuries, was the outcome of attempts to gain supremacy due to their extensive understanding of the sea routes and navigation achieved by their explorers. Each of the four countries deployed different strategies. One considered countries discovered as trading partners, another as endless supply of slaves and laborer's, and yet another used 'divide and conquer' to establish their rule. The target was to establish supremacy in spice trade, people trafficking or returning to the homeland with plundered loot – usually gems, gold and diamonds. The colonies were administered with an iron hand and often, mass human rights violations accompanied by the equivalent of war time looting was rampant under then existing laws, which could never have been acceptable for their own countries and people.

Loot, plunder and suppression or undue competitive leverage can only be an opportunistic strategy and can only last for a finite amount of time. Managing under such hostile conditions is extremely difficult and so by the turn of the twentieth century the voices within the colonialized nations became shriller and by the mid-twentieth century the four

European nations were no more empires; they had lost all their colonies except some minor ones.

As such, this is the declining or the *end-of-life-phase* market entry; focus needs to be on supporting products that are out of production or in extended maintenance of the support phase. These are for laggard customers who do not want to upgrade to anything new but are willing to pay exorbitantly for 'keeping the lights on' for their outdated products. The primary strategy is in pricing the support services significantly cheaper than what the original manufacturers provide. It is cut-throat, and often relies upon weaning the customer away from the original supplier. To combat this flight of customers, the OEMs need to have low and predictable costs to support these outdated products and continue to milk margins. But it is also a matter of time before these customers go away. Hence there is no sustained strategy to hold these customers forever. Examples are firms that support outdated releases of SAP and Oracle software. This stage is extremely opportunistic, and it is a matter of short time when the control over the customers will dwindle and the territories need to be vacated. There is truly little strategy needed.

The organizational product strategy based on the four realms of products lifecycle are – products of yesterday, products of today, products of tomorrow and products of the future. The appropriate organizational response and the likely pricing while developing and delivering the firm's products and offerings during various stages of its lifecycle is summarized in Table 4.5.

4.3 Time–Action Planning – Growing to Scale and Scaling to Grow

During a presentation of one of the three-year strategic business plans to the plc Board in London, the Chairman's first remark was, "Good, the plan has a lot of aspiration in

Table 4.5 Product Strategies across Four Realms of its Lifecycle

Product Focus Across Four Realms	Product Life Cycle Stage	Product Strategy	Organizational Response	Pricing Strategy
Future	Unfinished but early release	Disruptive solution	Rapid productization and market disruption	Significantly lower, subscription model
Tomorrow	Design/create	Invest	Innovate	Alpha customers – special price
Today	Early mover	Package	Specialized production	High pricing
Today	Growth	Variants	Mass production	Competitive pricing
Today	Maturity	Highly competitive	Feature addition	Commodity pricing
Today	Decline	Investments in next generation	Cost reduction	Discounted pricing
Yesterday	Extend	Support laggard customers	Specialized support	High priced maintenance
Yesterday	End of life	Order driven spares	Normally neglected support	Very high-priced spares/maintenance

it." He then continued, "How many people do you currently have?" and the headcount details were promptly given to him. "How many people will you have at the end of three years?" This time the projected headcount table was shown. The headcount was, of course, not increasing linearly with the increasing revenues; in fact, the differential between the increase in the headcount and the corresponding revenue increase was over 25% lower. "I am happy," the Chairman remarked, "Your business is scaling well!"

*

Growth, scale and scaling are interrelated terms. Growth means an increase in numbers, volume or size; growth is absolute. Scale is derived from measuring devices, like a 'graduated scale' and indicates a quantum, size or extent, especially when it is very big. Scale is relative. Scaling is the rate at which growth occurs. Let us take the example of a photograph having a specific dimension. If it were to be enlarged, a scale is needed to be applied to both its sides with an equal proportion. Such a scaling is referred to as 'linear scaling' in Euclidean geometry. Scaling can be 'non-linear' too; take, for example, a square photograph that is scaled by a factor of 2 on one side and a factor of 1 on the other, the result is a rectangular photograph. Scaling signifies the speed of change. Linear scaling represents constant speed of change while non-linear scaling is accelerating speed of change.

For a business to run optimally it must have a certain scale. For example, whether a restaurant has only a few customers visiting it or is running full, the chefs, the waiters, the manager and a minimum number of other team members are needed. Thus, the business must attract a certain minimum number of customers to cover the fixed costs; only beyond this does the restaurant generates profits. This is *growing the business to a certain scale* for it to perform optimally.

If the restaurant expands its operations by doubling the number of tables, it can now cater to double the number of customers. However, the additional staff needed is just a few – potentially only additional waiters. Thus, the quantum of cost increase is much less compared to the proportion of revenue increase. This is *scaling business* non-linearly via economies of scale. Hence growth, scale and scaling have three very distinct connotations, although they can sometimes be erroneously used interchangeably.

Linear scaling is of lower interest as it is synonymous to growth without any operational improvement. However, it is the non-linear scaling that is of utmost interest, and usually, whenever the business fraternity refers to scaling, they mean non-linear scaling (i.e., growth of revenues, with the costs tracking the revenues at a slower pace, and consequently generating higher overall profits). Scaling thus refers to the use of reduced resources whether it is time, effort, money, people or machinery, for a non-linear increased output. Scaling could also mean achieving desired outcome in a very short time.

Scaling up has received a lot of attention especially in the past few years. Numerous outstanding examples of scaling have been studied and diverse theories put forward. Although, many do's and don'ts are consistent, some of these theories seem to be quite contradictory signifying that one size does not fit all. There are many different approaches to scaling organizations, but each has a very situational relevance. Scaling up in a highly volatile situation and known-spaces means that it is impossible to hierarchically approve or sanction every decision, but since the risk is high, the most natural reaction is to set up additional bureaucratic processes with limited power of approval at every level. This situation is akin to a war where, it is the self-governance and clear-alignment that is more important than 'adding new processes and more scrutiny.' Sutton and Rao add that scaling should be slow and deliberate and should not be rolled out before the organization is ready for the change; this is especially true for medium and large organizations where higher inertia to change usually exists. Scaling, nevertheless, cannot be done without a committed and tireless team with clear alignment and well understood objectives.

Many, like Reid Hoffman, on the other hand, suggest a derivation from blitzkrieg – '*blitzscaling*,' to rapidly scale an organization in a very short time. In this mode, it is perfectly fine to push hard for hyper-growth even when the organization is not fully prepared and sometimes even when the roles are ill-defined – these situations obviously leave a lot of people unhappy, but beating time is assumed to be the biggest advantage here. Blitzscaling is thus most appropriate for volatile environments and for unknown spaces. Such a scaling strategy is usually deployed for start-ups and smaller organizations who are battling with the bigger corporations armed with new business models and blazing speed of execution but constrained by lack of time and ample cash.

With a population of 1.3 billion in India, scale and scaling have never been new to Indians. With customer segments from the ultra-poor to the uber-rich, similar products and services are available at significantly differentiated price points. Consequently, the features and/or quality of products across the entire scale varies significantly. One such example is of Indian IT organizations who have perfected the art of 'bottom-scaling' by keeping average salaries constant for years by hiring large batches of fresh graduates at starter salaries. Large scale hiring, tier four city operations, managing pyramids, rapid training with highly mature processes, automation, etc., have been used effectively for managing costs and scaling operations. And attritions higher up in the hierarchy are dealt by promoting from the high performing chain below. This is a method that is extremely suited to steady environments and own and known spaces.

Non-linear revenue generation has been a key component used for scaling revenues and this includes IP-based products, software platform-based strategy, etc. Acquisitions accelerate rapid customer acquisition scaling, which if not used judiciously, can end up in value destruction. One unique approach to rapid non-linear scaling is hinged upon the 10× rule, that many like Google and eBay have successfully adopted. If one were to scale their operations by ten times, then what would it look like? And to achieve that scale what needs to be done? The solution is not an incremental approach and hence requires breaking down every assumption, *as if bracing a business downturn.* One useful lever is to galvanize faster decision-making, e.g., adopting the mantra *"two iterations and just one more"* and if there is anything – a proposal, a presentation, decision-making process – that has not closed in two iterations, then everyone should come prepared to close it in the third. This strategy also reflects the American impatience that is encased in the maxim – 'two strikes and you're out.' This is a useful technique to bubble up all critical decisions not making headway. Another oft-used mantra is to plan for the final objective but with key milestones defined – like in a classic project management. This helps in surfacing many nuances that are needed to be taken care of – people, customers, shareholders, resources, etc., and even politics. The 10× method is scaling is extremely useful with steady environments for own, known and even unknown spaces. The scaling options are largely organization strategy and condition specific.

4.4 In Summary

■ Humans are torn between the anguish of past and the fear of future while ignoring the present. Organizations bask in the glory of the past and assume that the future is guaranteed. Both, however, need to make expedient use of the present to secure the future.

- Fulfilling 'needs' is immediate and warrants no strategy.
- The four states in the horizon of decision-making are strategic, tactical, operational and emergent–transactional action. Operationalization refers to commissioning and the pilot run.
- Emergent action if used objectively can spur breakthrough innovation.
- Lessons of market entry strategy can be drawn from the periods of Early Civilization (early movers), Empires (growth), Genocidal conquests (mature) and European colonialization (end of life).
- Successful strategy execution means complete understanding and alignment of key objectives flowing from top to down; most critical when teams are operating in volatile situations and a chain of command may not be available.
- Continuous monitoring of outcomes is critical and so are lead indicators.
- Running efficient operations means well-managed revenues, profits, growth from existing customers, acquisition of new customers, people engagement and innovation.
- Strategy is a set of broad options with meticulously identified outcomes and responses to those; execution is adherence to this well-detailed plan.

Chapter 5

Strategy Triangle Encirclements

Traps, Inhibitors and Competition Changers

Being ahead is not enough; being continuously ahead is critical. The Concorde supersonic commercial air aircraft even today remains the epitome of air travel. Commencing its first commercial operations way back in 1976, it was grounded after its last flight in 2003. A marvel in aero-engineering, the Concorde was a highly advanced aircraft with high caliber innovation for its time; but it had major shortcomings – a highly fuel inefficient, high maintenance, specialized aircraft catering to the elite few. An unfortunate crash in 2000 likely triggered the phasing out of the aircraft, downing with it the most talked about and exhilarating experience of flying between London and New York and arriving 'before you took off.' The manufacturers could have upgraded the aircraft but the cost of upgrade, especially baselining with the advances in aero-engineering over the 30 years of Concorde's existence, would have been so high that cost recovery from that stage onwards would have been impossible both for the manufacturer and its two airline users. In short, it was too little, too late, even for saving the most innovative and advanced engineering feat, far ahead of its time.

5.1 Strategy Encirclements and Strategy Inhibitors

One of the most often committed blunders that precipitates failure in a firm's evaluation of its strengths, weaknesses, opportunities and threats (SWOT) is that the *threats are underestimated* while the *strengths, overestimated*. These two coupled with a reckless and lethargic attitude give rise to misaligned responses and firms begin to miss registering threat signals from the market and unlikely competitors. Instead of phasing out anachronous products and business models, their current cash cows, they start investing into them hastening their advance to a certain death. The impact could lie anywhere between a sustained stall to a complete shutdown and business history is replete with such examples. The English language proverb that best mirrors this state is "too-little-too-late." The combined effect of this state with overestimated strengths and underestimated threats can be disastrous and is a strategy inhibitor.

The following 2 × 2 table (Table 5.1) encapsulates the impact of 'too-little-too-late' syndrome to overestimated strengths and underestimated threats.

The underestimated threats have a straightforward connotation – the threats are real, are building up and the firm is either ignorant of their existence or ignoring their impact on itself. When the firm's perception of the threat impact is low, it does precious little and is in the 'too little' phase. When the threat assumes reality culminating in a crippling impact on the firm, it is in the 'too late' phase.

Similarly, overestimated strengths, either due to the size of the firm or its market entrenchment, can engulf itself in a false sense of security. When a firm ignores changes in business

Table 5.1   Strategy Inhibitors – The Too-Little, Too-Late Syndrome

		Overestimated Strengths	
		To little (did not deploy)	*Too late (could not deploy)*
Underestimated Threats	Too little (low threat perception)	Lethargy Early exit	Changed rules of the game Too much effort needed to recover ground
	Too late (hit by full impact of the threat)	Marginalized On road to exit	Routed Forced exit

models and products being tested by its likely and unlikely competitors, and does nothing to protect itself, it is in the 'too little' phase. When the impact of such a change becomes real and crippling, and the firm is not able to deploy its resources as the change is irreversible, it is in the 'too late' phase.
The 'too little, too late' syndrome is akin to being *encircled*. Encirclement is an attack strategy that relies upon surrounding the enemy completely. Not only is it difficult for the enemy to escape but since all the supply lines are cut off, a wait-and-watch by the enemy only exacerbates the situation faster towards a bloody end.

The strategy triangles can be adapted to highlight such impending risks with a very simple overlay by drawing three concentric circles on the strategy triangles diagram with the center at the origin and circumscribing each of the three strategy triangles. It then visually depicts the firm under an encirclement attack, it also represents the degree of underestimation of threats, overestimation of strengths and misalignment of responses that the firm is exposed to. We call these 'strategy encirclements.' *The space axis represents overestimated strengths, the time axis represents underestimated threats and the action axis, misaligned responses.*

The space axis eerily also identifies the cause of misalignment – the innermost encirclement is due to own and self-inflicted causes; the middle encirclement is due to market and competitive reasons or known causes, and the outermost encirclement is due to unlikely candidates tearing apart established way of doing business thereby implying attack from the unknown – and the potential impact being very disruptive. The strategy encirclement is depicted in Figure 5.1.

The innermost circle or the *encirclement by self-incumbency* is a direct result of false sense of security and

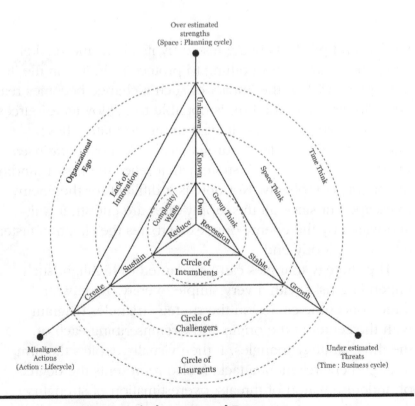

Figure 5.1   Strategy Encirclements and Entrapment

organizational lethargy. This sense of security is predicated upon the larger-than-life size of the firm, its brand name, its market share and penetration, deterioration in culture or complexity over time or anachronous internal business performance metrics that do not reflect changes in business environment. The degradation and lethargy set in and accumulate over time and in most cases the organization is not able to see itself in the slide until it is too late. Revising benchmarks and continually improving efficiencies, controlling costs and investing in employees is an absolute necessity. Companies need to adopt a mechanism for continual improvement.

The middle circle or the *encirclement by invaders (or challengers)* arises directly out of lack of organizational simplification and re-engineering at regular intervals, something the Harvard academician, Clayton Christensen, describes as sustaining innovation. The lack of sustaining innovation could be due to over dependence on a cash cow product or a few large revenue-generating customers. Sometimes underinvestment in products and relationships renders the firm uncompetitive as there are no deliberate plans for offsetting changing customer needs, or the aging underlying technologies or depreciating organizational capabilities.

The outermost circle or the *encirclement by insurgents* is the most difficult one to spot while in the making. It is triggered due to an extremely large organizational ego (not necessarily size alone) that fails to notice the breakdown of business models or the introduction of a disruptive product by a player who is usually very small and rarely very big. Insurgents use non-standard techniques and often they are not even sure as to the amount of change they can influence, or the damage they can inflict on their competitors. Usually they unleash a force that can be termed a *competition changer*. Competition changers are those inflection points in time when the fight moves from 'battling for today' to 'competing for the future.' However, before analyzing the competition changers, let us review how action, space and time axes can help avoid distortion and likely misreading the future, causing dysfunctional decision-making.

5.2 Avoiding Encirclement and Dysfunctional Decision-Making

Strategy formulation is not only a CEO's prerogative, it is a group activity. One of the biggest risks in any group activity is 'group think.' Irving Janis, the originator of the group think theory, studied many US foreign policy failures like the Bay of Pigs and concluded that very cohesive groups precipitate incorrect decisions due to lack of rigor in the decision-making process. This occurs primarily because personal viewpoint and dissent is sacrificed in favor of group consensus and avoidance of embarrassing the group. Group think is one of the strongest causes of precipitating encirclement of self-incumbency. The false sense of security is driven either by continuance of what has traditionally been followed or by the group taking the 'right' decision with dissenters being viewed as outside of the clique.

The action (on the action axis) is an outcome of decision-making post time and space considerations. Axis considerations are ignored or sometimes missed due to organizational ego, poor listening capabilities and group think. While group think is restricted to a cohesive group only and operates on the action axis of the strategy triangles model, incorrect decisions can also be taken on the other two axes of the strategy-triangles. These are termed 'space think' and 'time think' and used as extensions to group think.

Space think occurs when a group of organizations have a similar view of the future in their market space or segments and benchmark with each other to remain abreast with their peers. This is an inside-out view of themselves and their competitors. In space think, organizations miss reading unrelated information and transforming technology as change agents and impending competitors. They fail to realize that technological convergence could completely blur traditional boundaries and with it transform the price points, logistics of service delivery and atypical product features. Some of the examples worth mentioning are, Sony retired Walkman many years ago – who would have known that a computer maker, Apple, would have usurped its traditional music segment via the iPod? Nikon and Canon lost its lower-end market share for cameras to cell phone manufacturers; traditional security and surveillance systems manufacturers like Siemens, Bosch and Zicon faced an unlikely competitor, Cisco, who not only delivers remote home surveillance camera outputs via phones, but also helps in providing intelligent and smart homes. Cisco also supports heavy advances in remote surgery and medical sciences, something not its domain earlier. Space think operates on the space axis and is responsible for allowing encirclement by invaders; they are essentially 'domain invaders' and tend to blur lines between own and known, and, known and unknown. Since most of the invaders have a similar view of the future, the competition is a direct attack on the firm's products and services.

Time think can be defined as the inherent inconsistency that creeps in while studying reasons for success or failure of organizations within similar competitive time periods. Over time, the needs of consumers and the market dynamics changes, and, as mentioned earlier, 'a want today can become a need tomorrow.' Time and again analysts and researchers have made the mistake of identifying the reasons for success of top performing companies, only to their utter dismay watching the same companies disintegrate into nothingness – just because they missed the organization reaching stall points. The reasons are not incorrect but the needs and hence strategies of today are so different that they become irrelevant for sustaining the competition of future. Time think is the most deleterious of all as it allows rebels and non-conformists to creep up quietly, sometimes even without any self-realization of the intensity of disruption they themselves are unleashing – thus exemplifying encirclement by insurgents.

Time think is deleterious also when the firm is far ahead of its time and the existing ecosystem is inadequate to support such a solution. Every component needed for such an advanced solution needs to be created from grounds up. One example is that of a silicon-valley tech start-up Fabric7, which tried to anticipate what composable infrastructure is today, way back in 2006. We can think of such composability as a software-controlled mechanism through which network, compute, disk and memory capacity can be pooled together and parceled out in small chunks to multiple users. It was many years later, much after Fabric7 had folded their operations, that composable infrastructure appeared in its full vigor. Hence Time think can be harmful, both when firms are far ahead in their thinking, for a very ambitious scope, all by themselves but they are too small, or, when firms are too firmly locked up with a myopic view of the current period.

5.3 Competition Changers – Battling for Today, Competing for Tomorrow and Transforming the Future

Money spent on research and development is not necessarily the correct measure of how an organization is gearing up for tomorrow. Forward-looking companies invest about 10% of their revenues into research and development. Interestingly, while the money spent is reported under the heading 'research and development,' a large part of the outlay is on fixing defects or creating variants of the existing products – which effectively is battling for today only. True far-reaching research or investment in the future is really pursued by a select few essentially because the risks are much higher and returns not assured if one is second guessing the future.

The danger in blinking to the competition not only arises out of dated products and services, but more so out of breakdown of current business models and assumptions. The combination of immense advancements in technology and the digital highway that can transfer large masses of data over public networks is probably having the most telling effect in the way businesses are being conducted. Man has been able to digitize the first two of the five human senses completely, namely hearing and seeing, and can store and replicate the same with amazing fidelity; while the next three, touch, smell, and taste, are in extensive experimental stages.

Professional gear will always continue to exist for the highly discerning segment, but the making of movies and music, recording and processing, books publishing, medical devices and medical records management, etc., will continually evolve and change. The changes allow extremely advanced but inexpensive technology to be made available to create professional outputs and outcomes even by novices. Alternatively, exclusive experiences would be within the reach of the ordinary. Some examples would be Apple, which provides a rich array of apps for the creation of professional photos, movies, music or even ECG (electrocardiogram) heart monitoring with its watches, or SpaceX, which promises the experience of commercial space travel in the near future, or Uber, which could enable anyone with a car to be a taxi driver even in London without owning a black cab or having personal customers.

Our study has seen that organizations continuously evolve in four realms of time – the strategy for differentiating and battling for today, the strategy for seeding and competing for the tomorrow, the extremely restricted and short-term strategy for milking from the technologies and products of yesterday, but most importantly, the strategy for transforming the future. Some are successful, others not. However, it is the competition changers that organizations need to be watchful of as they alter the rules of doing business.

Competition changers may be defined as events that alter the competitive landscape of a market or a segment by shattering *space think and time think* and other constraining boundaries to redefine a product or service with significantly enhanced levels of delivery, product attributes, value, business model or price. Sometimes they slice the segment and many-a-times redefine the segment itself. Competition changers are always marked by distinctive pain triggers and extremely characteristics changes.

Competition can generally be viewed as a continuous stream of innovation across multiple time frames, punctuated by boundaries that are created by transformative and innovative technologies, disruptive products and models, and the ever-changing consumer needs. These boundaries are sign-posts of 'competition changers.' To simplify our discussion, we focus on current products and services in the contemporary time frame, near end-of-life products from the immediately preceding time span and on-the-anvil or future products designed for release in the succeeding time spans. We label them as today's competition, yesterday's competition and the future competition.

The convergence–divergence cycle: This is a phenomenon that is closely related to the economies of scope. It refers to the reduction in costs due to production of a variety of related products on the same assembly line, i.e., hamburger and fries (the most oft quoted), software products and customization services, etc., instead of just one. Convergence refers to the force multiplier achieved either by reusing the production, storage or logistical assets to produce multiple related products or by substantially increasing the versatility of a product by packing in advanced features and/or combining multiple product usage categories. Such products are general purpose and versatile in nature.

However, there always will, most definitively exist specialist requirements for very specific customer-segments, catered only by a standalone, best-in-class product and provisioned with expensive, highly specialized and discriminating features. These segments' requirements are so specific that a general product specification cannot support the entire width of product characteristics needed. Divergence refers to the research and production of such specialized products that continues in parallel with the general-purpose products.

One good example is the evolution of computer terminals. During antediluvian computing times, the old IBM and DEC mainframes had their own hardwired terminals. Each had their own port definitions, their own communication standard, their own proprietary VDU controllers and encryption methodologies. As computing evolved, researchers realized that it made no sense to have distinct hardwired terminals for every mainframe type and created the VT100 software-enabled terminals that could convert any desktop into a tele-typing terminal (aka tty). Thus, the communication standard between the computer and the terminal became standardized, although the software-enabled terminals continued to be directly connected to specific ports of the mainframe. As the Internet and local area networking progressed, researchers configured all hardware components (that included the mainframe computers and the terminals alike) on the same physical line, with every terminal having the ability to switch from one mainframe to another. The client-server era had just begun. Slowly the desktops that were emulating terminal behavior became so powerful that they started operating both as computing powerhouses as well as terminal emulators. Finally, the architecture of the application became so federated and distributed that no physical device was needed to act as a designated terminal. The application itself was split into a client, capable of human interaction, and a server that could process the client's request. The manufacturers of terminals had by now vanished – well almost. For most of the standard and general-purpose needs this was true; however, for more specific pure graphics needs, more advanced terminals with graphics accelerators were designed. Similarly, for restaurants, handheld terminals were created. This divergence of producing specific products based on the discerning needs and advanced specifications instead of using lower-cost, general-purpose products made more sense. Then Apple unleashed the smart devices and handheld terminals were quickly relegated to the Jurassic museum. Today smartphones have replaced both the computer as well as terminal power. The primary reason that precipitated the convergence above was the capability that allowed large blocks of data to be moved over large networks in packet switched modes. The convergence did not stop here.

The next were voice, picture and video – in fact, anything that could be digitized became a target of convergence. Cell phones began housing cameras, music systems, calculators and digital diaries. The economies of scope were in storing and managing digitized data. In each one of these, the convergence strategy was simple – create a competitive primary gadget (e.g., a cellular phone), bundled with general-purpose specifications of a widely used add-on product (i.e., a camera, calculator or a music player), thus increasing the perceived value and use enormously. Needless to say, ultra-discerning audiophiles and camera connoisseurs would continue to seek and pay enormous sums for these high-end specification standalone devices from the likes of Bose and Canon respectively.

Divergence occurs when converging technologies have bundled functionality that comes too close to the specifications of standalone product manufacturers. The most interesting example is the camera where the battle seems to be continuing interminably. The digital camera manufacturers completely killed analog camera producers and today the smartphone manufacturers seem to be on a similar collision course with the digital camera manufacturers – at least they have killed the lower end of the camera segment. Today, smartphones boast of having camera sensors with over 40 megapixels capacity. Canon, on the other hand, seemed to have a 250+ megapixels prototype sensor way back in 2015, although they are not certain they want to commercialize yet. Other areas like the wellness and fitness tracking devices, the satellite navigation-based devices, and 3D games are where the smartphones have attacked and conquered those domains too.

Convergence also becomes possible via extension. Remote surgeries are becoming state of the art now with a near-zero risk of losing life. Although this too uses the digital highway to move digitized data, the action is made possible by actuating extremely accurate mechanical arms. This class of convergence opens infinite possibilities. Advanced medical treatment is becoming available in remote corners of the world, frictionless payments and mobile wallets extend digital currency even to the poorest in remote villages, state of the art smart homes and smart appliances are becoming a pervasive existence around the globe, synchronized robots on faraway planets and outer space, distance education, MOOC (Massive Open Online Course) and collaborative research – the list is restricted only by the limits of our thinking. Convergence–divergence in the fast-changing modern technological world is thus one of the major innovation breeders that catalyzes competition changers.

Figure 5.2 emphasizes that a specification s_1 that is part of best in class product at time t_1, will find its way into the specifications of a general-purpose product at point in time, t_2. The hourglass representation is an additional view to convey that it is a matter of time before a general-purpose product specification (smartphone camera) catches up with what the best in class (SLR cameras) boasted of. The best in class, of course, needs to continuously stay ahead on innovation to keep the differentiation and the distance intact.

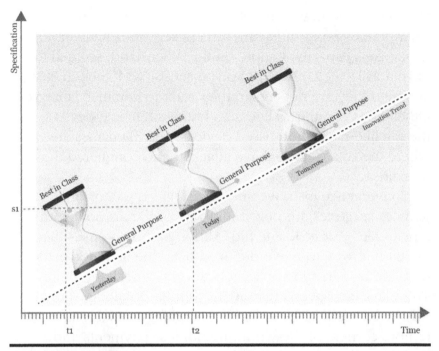

Figure 5.2   The Convergence–Divergence Effect – Specification Improvement Over Time

Another great example of the convergence–divergence phenomenon are the oscillations between pipeline and platforms business. Traditionally businesses were pipeline organizations till the platforms came in. Pipeline businesses started to move towards platforming their pipe while the platform business moved towards pipelining their platforms. Examples of the former are Nike, Walmart, John Deere or GoPro who are resorting to creating online platforms for engaging with their users, while examples of latter are Amazon and Walmart-Flipkart who are building physical stores to improve their offline presence.

Cost: This is the most fundamental reason for the emergence of competition changers. As society grows more prosperous over time, luxury becomes necessity and an unstated integral part of life. Increased consumption spurs competition, economies of scale, alternates, replacement products and the combined effect of all this is advanced features and technology at lower costs. Some great examples are free storage on the cloud, outcomes of attitudinal economics and, now, quantum computing.

Human pain: One of the biggest sources of competition changers arises from the quest to alleviate suffering, pain and disease. As societies grow more prosperous, people yearn to return their good fortune to the society – to the under privileged, to the sick and infirm, and to the needy; and this transcends race, geographical borders and bigot doctrines. If we are not united in sufferings, when can we be?

Molecular biology and study of genetics, isolation of genes that cause debilitating diseases like cancer, as well as those irritant factors that cause headaches are in well advanced stages of research. Such investments often spur the cutting edge of technology as well as research. One small but highly cutting-edge lab in New York is experimenting with non-corrosive, non-metallic magnets. This could revolutionize the way targeted drug delivery could be achieved inside the body.

The cause does not only end at battling for longevity and disease-free life. It also extends into economics and leading a respectful and dignified life – micro-finance is one such experiment that proved what small sums of money can do to uplift the under privileged and poor. Micro-financing also exploded the myth that only banks could borrow or lend.

Common global cause: Global population explosion is both, good and bad – good because population spurs consumption in a prosperous or a prospering economy; detrimental because indiscriminate use of technology that either harms the environmental fabric or accelerates consumption of scarce, rapidly depleting resources, precipitates irreversible destruction to living conditions. Some of these concerns are the depletion of ozone layer and global warming, carbon footprint reduction, harnessing ocean waves, solar and wind energies to generate power, green revolution, water scarcity, etc., to name a few.

Governments give impetus by way of tax concessions and research dollar funding, large corporations earmark funds and communicate their support in their annual reports; universities create coursework and fuel research programs and opportunity grabbers begin with investments into creating the products and services of the future.

Ownership on standards: The battle for creation and establishment of standards is considered key in defining and owning a product space. This is usually triggered by space think when two or more large corporations decide to define, own and invest in a future technology they both consider a technology changer (e.g., like the famous battle between Blu-ray versus HD technology). Obviously, such battles are expensive and only one finally wins. Such battles are fewer in number now.

5.4 The Digital Ecosystem – A Self-Sustaining Ecosystem?

All living organisms live in a habitat. Plants and animals together with non-living elements form an ecosystem. Not only landforms and air are non-living, but every living being too becomes non-living after its death. Plants are called producers as they produce food, animals including humans are called consumers as they consume food (herbivores eat plants while carnivores eat plants and animals); fungi and bacteria are called decomposers as they get their food from the dead and the decaying and converting them into minerals and nutrients that goes back into the soil to be consumed by the plants again. There are scavengers too who feed on the dead thus removing carcasses from the earth's surface and act faster than the decomposers. This *food chain* operates ceaselessly with the process of eating and being eaten – and maintaining a balance with no alarming excess of any single type in the ecosystem. Food chains are not only stand-alone but interconnected too and the network of such interconnected food chains is known as the food web.

Just like the universe is an ecosystem based on the food chain, the digital network is an ecosystem that is based on the *information chain*. Food implies energy and the food-chain energy flow; the food chain hence traces the energy pathway from the original source – the sun, to food producers (photosynthesis) to consumers and then the decomposers. Likewise, information is predicated on data and the information chain on the dataflow; the information chain traces its pathway from the originating data sources. The worldwide digital ecosystem is based on data creation and consumption. While the former (till not too long ago), had been limited to deliberate actions (i.e., data related to location, food, medicines, examination results, travel, portals, etc.), found their way to the worldwide digital ecosystem with a reason, the consumption of this data was in the form of information (or knowledge, via analysis) primarily for making informed decisions or transacting within the social, business or personal boundaries – again, all very purposeful and voluntary. With the advent of the digital ecosystem, as more and more devices are getting on the Internet, data creation is fast becoming an involuntary act. Devices are generating data related to non-living objects (cars, buildings, energy consumption, traffic, environmental conditions, etc.) as well as for living beings (health parameters, location, calories consumed, wellness, etc.) and can be consumed by making 'connections' out of this data (e.g., choice of route based on traffic conditions). Hence consumption too is now becoming an involuntary act – which means data that seemingly looks disparate may have many known and unknown connections and, when found, can help drive 'optimum' decision-making, reducing the ambiguous and the unknown. Automation, greater connectivity, big data storage, analytics, human-machine coordination and access to intelligent information by all will continue to drive this momentum.

A simple example like the digital boarding pass app always has up-to-date, current, continuously relevant data. If the flight is delayed the app automatically updates the new flight timings; it also knows which incoming flight will take off as the outgoing flight. Related businesses, which offer car pickup services, traffic monitoring services, airlines lounge services, lounge catering services, etc., can be connected via an unrelated 'intelligent' platform. Now, we have a small connected ecosystem. Connected ecosystems will drive the business models of the future instead of the current modes of the rigid vertical and horizontal integrations alone. They will no longer be restricted to the physical supply chain of their company but driven by the digital supply chain or their data supply chain like in the example above. Other example include education, which is already part of a connected ecosystem via common children data; so is health care and music industry via wearable devices. Traditional boundaries will continue to disintegrate, and new coalesced industry verticals will appear as an outcome of highly interconnected worldwide ecosystems.

Since data privacy is a very critical issue, not many 'scavengers' with unfettered access have surfaced. This has resulted in a technological race to store large quantum of data generated within and outside of the firm's boundaries. Going forward, over time, 'scavengers' that will free up unnecessary data will surface, even though platforms will continue to store such data of uninterested or dead people and devices, to draw accurate insights from the increased volumes of data. 'Personal scavengers' with access to deleting personal information held by such sites will potentially become legally valid and binding, disallowing abuse of personal data and metadata, something rampant today. Intelligent 'decomposers' have already surfaced, which have the analytical capability of decomposing and connecting large masses of data to reveal deep insight, thus making human life much better in nearly every field. This decomposed insight goes back into intelligent and learning systems to improve their behavior and make it smarter and more human like.

With such an increased proliferation in the adoption of digital highway, solutions will emanate that will greatly enhance collaboration and efficiency within government, business and personal areas alike. The worldwide digital ecosystem will be very similar to the food web. Just as a Michelin-star chef cooks and presents a gourmet meal matched both visually as well as in taste, in the digital world focus on 'user experience', deep design and service design, will continue to retain its preeminent importance. User experience could be explicit (i.e., a digital library through an immersive virtual reality with access to millions of books sitting at home); or very subtle (e.g., an ingestible device that monitors and regulates body parameters automatically and dials out to a personal doctor if the parameters exceed the pre-set limits). The machines and devices will be self-learning and based on deduction by 'intelligent decomposers' from the mass of data available. Future life thus will be very connected and at the risk of sounding paranoid, potentially exposed and intrusive.

5.5 In Summary

- Battling for today and tomorrow is guided by competition changers. The convergence–divergence cycle traces cutting-edge innovation in general across industries and is responsible for the battle on the digital highway.
- Cost, human pain, common global cause, fight for ownership of standards and digital ecosystem are some of the main catalysts for competition changers.
- The digital ecosystem is analogous to the universe as an ecosystem; while the universe is based on the food-chain cycle, the digital ecosystem is based on

the *information-chain* cycle. Food signifies energy and hence the food chain traces the energy pathway from the sun; information is predicated on data and the information-chain traces the data-flow.

■ So far, the digital ecosystem was based on deliberate, purposeful and intentional data creation and consumption. In the new age of the digital ecosystem, data creation is becoming an involuntary act and consumption, intrusively insightful.

Selected Bibliography – Section II

Bose, Partha. 2003, *Alexander the Great's Art of Strategy*, Penguin Books.

Clausewitz, Carl von. 1873, *On War*, English translation, Oxford World's Classics, 2009.

Clavell, James. (Trans, Ed.) 1983, *The Art of War by Sun Tzu*, Delacorte Press.

Ibrahim, Ahmed. 2006, *Western Civilization from 1500*, HarperCollins Publishers.

Kautilya. 1992, *The Arthashastra*, Translated and Edited by Rangarajan, L.N., Penguin Books.

Keay, John. 2008, *China – A History*, HarperCollins Publishers.

Man, John. 2005, *Genghis Khan – Life, death and Resurrection*, Bantam Books.

Sullivan, Tim. April 2016, Blitzscaling – An interview with Reid Hoffman, *Harvard Business Review*.

Sutton, Robert I. and Rao, Huggy. 2014, *Scaling Up Excellence*, Penguin Random House.

Vasconcellos, Dr. Jorge. 2003, *Strategy Moves*, Financial Times/ Prentice Hall.

Strategy Triangles

Driving Business Performance and Transformations in a Continuously Evolving Business Environment

"Life looks for life."

– Carl Sagan

Chapter 6

Strategy Triangles and the Evolutionary Cycles on the Earth

The evolution of a firm is no different from the evolution of life on this planet. In fact, Geoffrey West's comparative studies on the scaling of biological species, firms and urban cities gives scientific proof that if firms don't innovate, they will wither away and die.

It was not only West who compared organizations to living beings but also Richard Pascale. Pascale likened organizations to "complex adaptive systems," which could learn from the past and recognize patterns to predict the future. He postulated a few core principles universally applicable to all such systems. For starters, equilibrium foreshadows death for any complex adaptable system; this is also a confirmation of West's thesis on firms that do not innovate. These systems have the intelligence to evolve from simple structures to more complex ones as they grow and exhibit self-organization over time. Once they have achieved a temporary peak, they must necessarily 'go down' for them to scale back up again. Controlled instability, also termed as 'the edge of chaos,' is a catalyst that activates evolution; controlled instability implies competition, macro-economic shocks, technology disruptions, and impulse and attitudinal economics. If the instability is uncontrolled, the result is a chaos. Finally, "complex adaptive systems cannot be directed but only disturbed" (i.e., outcomes cannot be guaranteed based on inputs alone). These postulates further establish that a firm is a living being. But can it use the same levers that nature does? The readers will not only see that there is a very close parallel but will be presented with numerous examples and anecdotes in this section.

The greatest crisis that ever occurred on the earth was about 251 million years ago when over 90% of the then existing species became extinct. Extinction of species on earth is a regular feature of evolution, but mass extinctions, like the one which occurred 251 million years ago, ends up in a huge spike of extinctions over very short periods. The prime reason for the precipitation of such catastrophic events, scientists believe, was due to dramatic climatic changes. So far, over the past four-and-a-half billion years of earth's existence, there have just been five events of mass extinction. Alarming and devastating as it may sound, the empty niches such large-scale extinctions leave behind are filled by new families, giving rise to an increased bio-diversity of life on the earth. In fact, they trigger an increased rate of evolution. This is nature's way of eliminating the rigid and non-adaptable life forms. So far 99% of all species that ever-occupied earth, amounting to 5 billion, are extinct. Evolution is just a regular weeding phenomenon within nature's repertoire of actions.

The earth, according to scientists, was born about 4.6 billion years ago out of solar dust that created the entire solar system. It was uninhabitable then, without any oxygen, and punctuated by frequent volcanic activities and magnetic storms. Life was impossible. However, life's resilience was so remarkable that even under such impossible circumstances, it found a slightly hospitable nook, and consequently, the first life in its most primitive form surfaced on our planet – our common universal ancestor.

In work by John Sutherland of the Cambridge University, Sukrit Ranjan of MIT, and later Thomas Carrel of Ludwig-Maximilians-Universität München, the answer seems to at least partially lie in sulfidic anions, likely found in the lakes and shallow water bodies on early earth. These ions participated in chemical reactions that converted the prebiotic molecules into the building blocks of RNA, proposed as the first molecule of life. This was earth's initial phase of creation or the first phase of nature's innovation. Multicellular forms evolved a billion years later, and it was not until about 570 million years ago that a wider variety of lifeforms started to evolve. By this time the environment had become more hospitable and stable enough to support a large diversity of lifeforms.

Next, came the phase of genetic mutations or genetic variation, which can be easily summed up as natural genetic re-engineering. The evolution from the first unicellular life to the current biodiversity is the result of genetic mutations. Genetic movement materializes via two mechanisms, the vertical gene transfer and the horizontal gene transfer. The vertical gene transfer occurs when the species collect traits during their life span and transfer them to their offspring through the process of reproduction. The genomes interact with the environment continuously to cause changes in some of the heritable traits through genetic mutations. Natural selection then identifies the most robust genes for being passed to the generations below. This causes a specific population of species to survive and reproduce more, while other not-so-sturdy species to wither away – aka the law of natural selection. The horizontal gene transfer, on the other hand, is the process by which genetic material is transferred from one organism to another but without being its offspring, like in bacteria.

The last phase in the continuous cycle of evolution is the phase of extinctions and these are not sudden events. They usually build up over years, sometimes thousands of years, accumulated due to lethargy in response to changing environment or due to a predator that a species was not able to cope with. While the law of natural selection emotionlessly keeps weeding out the weak and the poorly-adjusted, nature does give another interesting mechanism, *epigenetics*, to help counter the adverse effects of environmental stress. Cells in a living being have the same gene sequence but can yet perform different functions (e.g., liver, brain or heart cells). This is because each cell type has a different combination of genes that are activated to enable the specific function. This is achieved via a signal that can switch off or switch on these gene groups also known as *epigenetic* mechanism. Epigenetics takes anxiety caused by environmental factors like diet, stress, habitat or lifestyle as continuous inputs and regulates the gene expression by switching it off (e.g., to ignore the anxiety), without mutating the gene itself. It prepares the species better for future occurrence of such stress-inducing conditions. The epigenetic markers were so far considered to be non-hereditary. However, the latest research shows that even epigenetic changes are heritable (i.e., under stressful environment conditions the body uses epigenetic markers not only to respond to the stress but can also pass the same to its progenies).

Returning to the mass extinctions, they were very important events as they triggered lifeform transformations. The species that became extinct just vanished; others that survived evolved into something quite different in their next phase of evolution. For example, scientists believe that birds are descendants of dinosaurs. Although dinosaurs became extinct in the last event, it was the smallest form weighing less than one kilo that survived, possibly because of its ability to adapt and change. Similarly, amphibians evolved from fish and reptiles across multiple events. Humans evolved from the primates. Evolution is thus an endless cycle of new species being born, then being developed over millions of years via genetic mutations, many becoming extinct due to their inability to respond to drastic climatic changes, and, finally, a few variants of those extinct species being transformed into something more adaptable and different. The cycle of evolution continues to work tirelessly.

Applying the strategy triangles principles to the evolutionary cycle on earth, the fundamental variables (i.e., the space, time and action axes) appear as depicted in Figure 6.1.

The time axis depicts the climatic cycle. It swings from being *'climatically formative'* – in some areas of the earth, to *'climatically conducive'* and finally to *'climatically difficult.'* It is important to note here that climatically difficult may not necessarily mean a pervasive degradation in the environment for all organisms on the earth but more than likely within localized environments (e.g., increased global warming could increase the temperature of the Arctic sea thus causing irreversible marine damage to the sea-life there).

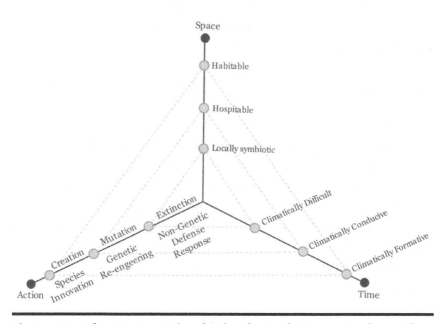

Figure 6.1   The Strategy Triangles for the Evolutionary Cycles on the Earth

The space axis represents the earth in its entirety. The 'habitable' sub-territory are all spaces on the earth where life can exist. 'Hospitable' spaces are those where life can prosper with a variety of flora and fauna established. Finally, the 'symbiotic habitats' are spaces where there is an excellent balance of symbiotic relationship between all the living beings – big or small. These are also the natural environments where specific species can easily live in.

The action axis represents nature's cycle of evolution through the stages of creation, evolution via genetic mutation, and, finally, extinction of the species. The creation phase is nature's *innovation* phase. The genetic variation or mutation phase is evolution's *re-engineering* phase that helps in battling the effects of environmental changes over longer time scales. The extinction phase is the *continual improvement* phase – or survival of the fittest, for those organisms that can combat and adjust to the environmental changes, while for the weak species, it is extermination. Epigenetic markers are tools that nature provides to the organisms in this phase to continually combat and respond to environment changes in the short term. Finally, *transformation* occurs when an entire specie becomes extinct except for a small quantum of a more responsive variant that survives and goes on to evolve into something very different and nimble, like the example of evolution of birds from dinosaurs.

It is near certain that the organisms that are well settled within the confines of their habitats and find it difficult to respond to deteriorating environmental changes, are on nature's checklist for self-extermination. If the environmental degradation is very slow then the likelihood of the species' response to the change will be very poor, especially in the short term, and could be highly impaired in the long term. This is true for firms too. The equivalent strategy triangles diagram thus for organizational evolution, as will be seen, would exactly superimpose on the nature's mechanism of evolution. However, it is not all jungle only – what is missed many a times is that cooperation is a vital strategy in nature. Cooperation is what creates a symbiotic habitat.

*

It was in the eighties when studies on performance improvement of firms picked up steam. Over the ensuing 40 years research on continual improvement, re-engineering and innovation found their way into management edifices and boards, mostly triggered by the increased rate of demise of rock-solid companies, largely due to their rigidity and the inability to rapidly respond to change or drive innovation. Management boards and consultants began to use the term 'transformation' very loosely and interchangeably with the above three to denote organizational change. However, the four have very distinct connotation and can be differentiated elegantly using the mechanism of evolution and STA strategy triangles.

Firms' performance improvement levers correspond very closely to the levers of nature's evolution. These four different mechanisms that can be applied across the lifecycle states of a firm (i.e., continual improvement, re-engineering, innovation and transformations) correspond to non-genetic defense mechanisms, genetic re-engineering, species innovation and the combination of extinction followed by species innovation. While the methodologies and outcomes of the first three are well documented for catalyzing sustained business performance, the last one – transformations, is either referenced colloquially or is diffused, both in its definition as well its methodology. Transformations are like powerful transmutations that can metamorphose a firm, an environment, or a relationship into something fresh and new. Transformation implies pain and change but may not always be disruptive. It could be generative too and rewarding for everyone. The subsequent chapters discuss in detail its applicability and implications as well as removes misconception and vagueness from its definition, characterization, implementation and outcomes. But let us first cover the first three levers.

6.1 In Summary

- The evolution of a firm is no different from the evolution of life on this planet.
- The STA strategy triangles principles can be applied to the evolutionary cycles on the earth.
  - The time axis depicts the climatic cycle and swings between 'climatically formative' to 'climatically conducive' to 'climatically difficult'.
  - The space axis represents how habitable the earth is and lies between habitable, hospitable and locally symbiotic.
  - The action axis represents nature's evolution cycle between the stages of species creation, genetic variation and mutation, epigenetics, and, finally, the extinction of the species.
  - Transformation occurs when a species becomes extinct except for a small quantum of responsive variant that survive and evolve into something very strong and different.
- The equivalent STA triangles diagram for the evolution of the firm is identical. The equivalent continuum on the action axis for
  - Species creation, genetic mutation and species extinction corresponding to organizational innovation, re-engineering and continual improvement.
  - Transformation is the same – rebirth after extinction.

Chapter 7

Driving Business Performance

The Progression of Continual Improvement, Re-engineering and Innovation

7.1 A Simple Framework for Managing Change

The business environment is volatile and rapidly changing and organizations are confronted with the task of regular remedial responses in order to maintain its position and growth. With organizations getting bombarded by such a constant stream of multi-dimensional change, an effective change management strategy is needed.

Change can be intentional or unintentional; it could also be welcome or unwelcome. Change thus can be categorized into three key types. When change is intentional, though it may not always be welcome, it needs to be reinforced and carefully managed. When change is unintentional and unwelcome, it needs to be combated and reversed. There are also the rare occurrences when change is unintentional but welcome. Such a change usually catalyzes hope and transformations. Any change not managed well can wreak chaos. Chaos signifies loss of rhythm; usually shock waves, unpreparedness or detractors cause loss of organizational rhythm and consequently chaos.

Rhythm, perturbations, change and chaos are very closely and sequentially linked. Rhythm is the essence of everything in nature and according to Lefebvre, is anything repetitive with strong and weak times. Hence it is characterized by patterns and movements with highs and lows within it. Rhythm gets altered, and in extreme cases broken, by perturbations. Perturbations are the result of external forces that either accompanies natural degradation with passage of time or causes an unintended or intended change. Perturbations cause path deviations. It can cause minor deviations, major deviations or even chaos. For example, ocean waves exhibit rhythm; but when an ongoing wave from the ocean meets a returning wave from the shore, it breaks into a chaos due to turbulence, reversals and unpreparedness.

Businesses ride through the highs and lows of their business cycles and hence become part of the business rhythm. Change gets injected due to perturbations caused by competition, consumption, regulations, high-growth or deterioration with their impact ranging from the minor to major to pure chaos. Businesses can either be impacted by such a change or else can be the cause of such a change. In both the cases change needs to be very meticulously managed. The STA triangle aids effectively in categorizing key types of changes. It also helps in processing the change management itself.

Combating change for 'bringing systems back to the equilibrium state': Such changes are triggered by internal breakdown and outages in plant and machinery, organizational processes, and relationships with employees, customers or stakeholders. The intent is to quickly restore the operational state and such situations correspond to 'emergent or transactional' rapid-responses needed to combat aberrant occurrences. Organizations usually set control limits and employ proactive care to remain within these boundaries by adopting preventive maintenance schedules, employee and customer surveys, and certifying their operations against standards like ISO or CMMi. This, therefore, corresponds to 'optimization' or simplification on the action axis of the STA triangle and focusses on organizational *systems*. It drives 'organizational maintenance.'

Driving change for 'increased throughput and sustained organizational equilibrium': Such changes are triggered by increased need for significant enhancement in internal and external organizational metrics, usually benchmarked against the best in the industry. These include financial metrics, people metrics and operational metrics. Such change programs are usually sponsored by the top management, are persistent for a specific duration, have a budget, have planned outcomes and a defined target end-state. Usually execution of such programs is also accompanied with the by-product of improved organizational equilibrium and hence reduced breakdowns and outages. This management of change is related to 'organizational sustenance' and corresponds to 'preservation' on the action axis of the STA triangle. It is focused on organization *behavior* and helps in the creation of new variants from the existing, whether products, strategy or process.

Leading change for 'increased innovation and sustained organizational transformation': Such changes are triggered by the need for innovation and transformation for driving cutting edge disruptions in the market, maintaining a market lead and in general to achieve an all-round success in a continuously changing business environment. Usually this involves creating an environment of trust, multi-way communication and empowerment within the organization and is predicated on a strong view of the future, a budget for failure and the creation of the new. The organization is not always certain of the exact end-state that it would have achieved through its disruptions nor it is sure of the extent of impact that it could create in the market. This thus corresponds to 'organizational innovation and transformation' on the action axis of the STA triangle and needs a strong *culture* of the organization as the prime mover.

Both, the art of managing change as well as the levers for scaling performance are needed ultimately for driving a leadership position and are strongly intermeshed. While both can be superimposed on the action axis, the latter has its foundations on the gradation of change as adopted by the natural evolutionary cycles, and the former is based on the art of skillfully managing the process of change itself, and its impact on the organization.

7.2 Deploying Continual Improvement, Re-engineering and Innovation

Continual improvement, re-engineering and innovation in business can be viewed as a continuum on the action axis, identical to nature's mechanisms of evolution. These three could be used effectively, either non-exclusively or in parallel, as levers that drive multiple change strategies capable of achieving effective force multipliers when aggregated.

Continual improvement implies reduction, optimization or simplification on the action axis and corresponds to the 'destruction' state. It can be used, for example, to deliver incremental features in an existing product driven by the changing needs of the market. It can also be applied for driving incremental output or incremental efficiency, continuously; or it could be used in driving Six Sigma improvements to repetitive operations. Continual improvement is analogous to *incremental or sustaining innovation*. However, this should not be confused with incremental impact. In fact, the impact could be anywhere from minimal to nothing short of awe inspiring.

An elegant instance of improvement that impacted just a single person, yet had a substantive impact on the overall system, was at the headquarters of a global organization. The use case may not be as relevant today, but the beauty of critical thinking is. Being the global headquarters meant that all function heads like Corporate Finance, Corporate Strategy, Marketing, Human Resources, and the Managing Director's office were on the same floor. The office boy (if we could use this term), had the task of moving all box files at the end of the day from multiple tables, back to dedicated file racks allocated to the respective functions. Unfortunately, it was taking quite a while for the office boy, after office hours, as he had to read each file and place it in the right rack-shelf, sequenced alphabetically. A simple visual intelligence was introduced to help the office boy perform his task with substantial ease. First, a small movable trolley was introduced that the office boy could use to collect and move the files to the respective rack stands – a commonsense step. Next, the shelves on each of the racks were painted with a unique color assigned for each of the five functional groups – blue for the MD's office, yellow for HR and so forth (each rack was a cupboard with five shelves with the box files kept from the top left of the first shelf to the bottom right of the last shelf in ascending alphabetical sequence). Next, with all the files of the respective functions arranged in their respective stacks, colored pens, the same as the shelf color, were used to draw diagonal lines from the top left to the bottom right of each shelf. The first shelf had one line running as a diagonal across the box files; the second shelf had two thin parallel lines, the third shelf three, the fourth shelf four and the last shelf five. This configuration made it extremely efficient and easy for the office boy. Once he had collected all the files he would roll the trolley to the shelf, pick out all the files with lines of the same color as the shelf color, place the files on the shelf – single-line files on the first shelf, double-lined files on the second and so on – and finally recreate the diagonal line visually in each shelf by moving the files around. Needless to reiterate, the files needed to be in a specific singular order to recreate the diagonal. While the example may have looked like a mathematical puzzle, the impact was particularly spectacular for the office boy. The solution is equally usable for setting up filing for any office, especially if there are no office boys, in line with our thinking of reducing waste. Continual improvement reflects incremental change that not only impacts businesses but also human lives, sometimes even for the lowest in the hierarchy of the firm. Needless to add, this is still a fully functional idea, and can be used whether one has a shelf, a cupboard or multiple cupboards to stack box files alphabetically.

Another befitting example is the British cycle team that came from nowhere to becoming the world champions by aggregating results from several incremental improvements to achieve a disproportionate outcome. Between 1908 and 2003, the British cycling team had won only one gold medal at the Olympics, and, worse, no British cyclist had ever won the coveted Tour de France medal. Sir David John Brailsford was appointed as the performance director for the professional British cycle team in 2004. His approach was to affect an improvement of just 1% in everything obvious or unobvious that could positively impact the performance of the cyclist. Everything from seats to gears, gels, disinfectants, to keeping away simple infections like colds and coughs, and even travelling with pillows that the cyclists used at home and could help them get a good night's sleep before the competitive event, became part of the 'kit.' Within five years of Dave Brailsford taking over the team, Great Britain went on to become a dominating force in the category and, as of today, holds hundreds of cyclist medals under its belt – Olympics and Tour de France included. This is a great example of how extraordinary gains can be achieved by aggregation of very incremental improvements across every conceivable factor that could have an enormous impact on the overall performance.

*

Re-engineering, on the other hand, relates to process and workflow redesign – the act of 'resequencing' on the action axis and corresponding to the 'sustenance' state. Re-engineering is also loosely referred to as *process innovation*. When Hammer and Champy introduced it in the nineties, they defined it as "the fundamental rethinking and radical redesign of business processes to bring about dramatic improvements in performance." It wasn't just about optimization. Re-engineering based its core tenets on efficiency, reduced waste and increased throughput.

- First, it considers any 'hands-off time' or the time taken between process steps, i.e., moving from the end of a step to the beginning of the next step, as waste, whether it is paper being pushed or an actor unaware of a task waiting for him. The most common mechanism to get rid of unnecessary wait times, is automation.
- Second, it also attacks superfluous and inefficient iterations while doing the actual task – or within the 'hands-on' time. It views multiple handoffs between two persons or departments as inefficient and wasteful – even if it is to collect data and take decisions iteratively. Re-engineering has thus resulted in changes in layouts of the shop floor (in one case to get the washrooms in the center just to reduce the operator down time in walking to the toilets), or changes in the way loans and mortgages are processed to greatly improve their response times.
- Third, automation is also used to reduce hands-on time when the process is highly repetitive or

outcomes predictable. Today, software bots are regularly deployed for reducing multiple entry of the same data across screens or applications, saving time and precious human effort; chatbots have been deployed to account for intelligent customer engagement during off-peak as well as very high peak loads to supplement human agents.

One of the biggest success stories of re-engineering that has achieved quantum results is improving the entire software development process from the traditional waterfall to the agile development process. Instead of development and testing being two separate engagements at two different slots of time significantly apart, the agile software development methodology brought these two together thus reducing the lag between writing code, and finding and fixing defects, which was usually done at the end of the waterfall development cycle. Re-emphasizing, the impact can again be incremental or monumental, as characterized in the examples below.

An early example is Dell applying the postponement strategy to implement the famed merge-in-transit supply-chain process for dealing effectively with the wide configuration of products that they were shipping. The idea was to delay the final assembly to a final merge point where all the suppliers would ship the variable components (memory, drives, controllers, etc.) of the ordered capacity. This increased the speed of assembly and shipments and at the same time allowed for virtually any customer-requested PC configuration. Today, a parcel–delivery–runner start-up uses this with a minor variation to deliver packages from one point to another. Runners are on routes that commonly intersect where they exchange packets as they cross each other in transit. If the transit match is not possible, then they extend the runner to deliver to the final point, which is not a frequent occurrence.

Buying fashion accessories and clothing on ecommerce sites has triggered a unique behavior globally. A friend's wife in London uses the service as if she were in a real store – she orders a dozen items of clothing, selects two from them and return ships the rest. In a specific state in India, this was being extended even further to non-ethical limits. People would order expensive clothing, wear it for the occasion needed, and then use the 30-day return policy to send back the used clothes and ask for refund. Myntra, a fashion ecommerce company, re-engineered their 'returns' workflow by introducing the 'try and buy' service to their customers, which allowed genuine buyers a trial to check the body fit of the clothes but reduced significantly the fraudulent instances of using and then returning the used clothing. Another change they introduced was an inspection and the right to reject if any clothing looked used or was without labels in a genuine return. The simple re-engineered process saved Myntra both money as well as causing a significant reduction in fraudulent claims.

A great example of an extremely complex re-engineering cited earlier in the book was of Reliance, which re-engineered the plant erection process, in complete variance to the then established methods, to deliver the Jamnagar refinery in nearly half the initially projected time.

*

Innovation refers to something new being born. Innovation means making changes to something established, especially by introducing new methods, ideas or products. Innovation can also be a by-product of failed experiments, or an outcome of dealing with pain, shortages, substitution, constraints, limitations or consolidation. Innovation thus means change and disruption. With continual improvement and re-engineering an equivalent to *incremental innovation* and *process innovation* respectively, innovation in the native form on the action axis is termed as *breakthrough or disruptive innovation* and corresponds to the 'creation' state. Many studies have tried to understand the science behind successful innovation across the entire innovation value chain. It usually begins with an overflowing hopper of ideas with a sharp focus on ideation, as the greater the number of ideas in the hopper, the more likely chances of encountering a breakthrough idea. Disruptive innovations are a direct result of competition changers; they creep up behind and, as if triggering a domino, they give no time to the competition to respond. It is an interplay of technology, evolved needs and exponentially better outcomes.

There are numerous examples of innovation, from the blue ocean strategy, e.g., Yellow Tail used the simple innovation of changing the wine cork to a cap and at the same time targeted beer drinkers to disrupt the deeply entrenched native Australian wine manufacturers; to Clayton Christensen's research on disruptive innovation and a number of examples that followed the theory; or the theory of exponential growth

Table 7.1 How Can Companies Continuously Innovate?

		Shattering Time Think	
		Customer insights available	*Customer unaware of such a need*
Shattering Space Think	Atypical products and features	Creating new demand (e.g., blue ocean strategy)	Exponential growth curve or tipping point
	Convergence in technologies or cross-domain applicability	Disruption (Christensen's)	Transformation

and the tipping point – which highlights that till the tipping point is reached the growth is arduous, and post that point it rises exponentially. A well-funded organization listening and responding to its customers carefully will finally see the tipping point (or the exponential uplift) – Tesla, Intuit or Paytm. However, smaller companies with limited cash use pivots to exit and change because their very survival is at stake. This is analogous to stock traders using exit criteria diligently, as the prime aim is to protect the principal. Innovation needs organizations to be highly disciplined. Although mass scale disruption cannot be pre-planned, in larger companies innovation usually is a process with stage-gates. In smaller companies, pivot is usually a good reality check.

How can companies continue to innovate? The 2 × 2 (Figure 7.1) depicts the approach to do so. The x-axis depicts mechanisms to shatter time think and the y-axis, space think. Breaking out of the clutches of time think relies upon deep customer insight reflecting the *changing future needs* or establishing new needs, that sometimes even the customer is unaware of. Breaking space think relies upon atypical products and features or when traditional boundaries merge and creating new competition.

As time changes so do the needs of the consumers – and hence continuous customer insight is needed for innovating beyond the current competitive period. The iPhone itself was an outcome of this process – it had such atypical features and capabilities that no competing phone at that point in time had. It wiped out all the cell-phone manufacturers of that era; only one survived, which had rapidly resorted to matching their product characteristics to that of the iPhone, the new benchmark. It was an outcome of a blue ocean strategy. In fact, several Chinese copies are thriving very well in the market today, until yet another competition changer arrives and destroys the party.

When customer insight or pain is applied to technological convergence, new competitors appear that transgress traditional domains. Cisco entered the medical and smart home space, Uber unionized taxis, and Airbnb, traditional hoteling. This quadrant is a classic example of Christensen's disruptive innovation.

When the customer need is unestablished and atypical products are launched, innovation adoption is slow initially but beyond a tipping point causes exponential growth. This category has many examples like photocopiers, personal computers, autonomous cars and ecommerce website usage. This is the quadrant of exponential growth or the tipping point.

Finally, the last quadrant is of a product in a cash-cow or end-of-life stage that likely needs to be killed to be reborn into something very different. The rebirth is either the previous features subsumed into something new or generated from radical thinking. It could also be something never thought of before. The solution could be as radical as a robot on a PE firm's board, or the creation of the Internet itself, or the cloud services and the 3D printers. It could also be iPod features subsumed by the iPhone. This is the quadrant of transformations.

Why does Apple appear to be running out of steam in innovating its products? Apple seems to be imprisoned in a state of time think – and is now only adding features to a successful product that it created in 2008. Should it follow the path of its illustrious founder of killing the product before the market does it for them and create the next product that subsumes the iPhone? That will need a transformation, which the next chapter dives deeply into.

*

A final clarification. Tipping point as a phenomenon is not only unique to technical innovation. It is applicable to normal life occurrences, the draw of luck, probability theory and even transformations. Take, for example, the first instance of the

Black Death or the deadly bubonic plague, which reached the European continent at Crimea from central Asia in 1343. In the ensuing eight years, the pandemic killed an estimated 75 to 200 million people in Eurasia, the largest incidence of deaths ever encountered in an pandemic in the history of human mankind. Although the pervasive impact of the affliction ebbed, the deadly bacteria kept coming back in the ensuing years across many centuries till it marked a retreat in the eighteenth century from Europe and the nineteenth century from Africa. Instances of the pandemic continued to pulverize Asia and even North America in the twentieth century. It was only in 1894, nearly 550 years after Europe saw this deadly disease for the first time, that the bacterium was isolated and cultured by Alexandre Yersin in Hong Kong, and later in 1898 Paul-Louis Simond discovered that the bacterium was transmitted from rodents by flea bites. The treatment was found for the first time in 1896, although experimentation on the development of vaccines and antigens continued until the twentieth century.

The Ebola virus disease was first identified in 1976 near the Ebola river in Africa. This was a very high risk-of-death disease and the worst outbreak that occurred was between 2013 and 2016 in Western Africa where many died. By December 2016, a vaccine had been developed for the disease and as of now the disease is completely under control.

In June 2009, the World Health Organization had declared swine flu or H1N1 as a pandemic; in August 2010, it had declared the disease as seasonal and completely under medical control. The speed of response under chaos has dramatically improved.

Science and scientific thinking were hamstrung with the slow speed of research and innovation in earlier centuries simply because the core postulates had not yet been discovered. It reached the 'tipping point' towards the end of the nineteenth century, after which the speed of new research and expansion into new frontiers of science and even the arts exploded. Communication and travel brought communities together and distributed research flourished. Today the medical responses to newer and deadlier mutations of epidemic causing diseases are much quicker and the international community joins hands to contain, control and prevent occurrences of such diseases. These are instances of breaking free of time think and adopting generative transformations, something that we will soon see.

This was also the story of Fabric7, caught in the time think, that we touched upon earlier.

7.3 In Summary

- Change can be intentional or unintentional; and, welcome or unwelcome.
  - When change is intentional, though it may not always be welcome, it needs to be reinforced and carefully managed.
  - When change is unintentional and unwelcome, it needs to be combated and reversed.
  - When change is unintentional but welcome, it reflects hope and transformation.
- Rhythm, perturbations, change and chaos are very closely and sequentially linked.
  - Rhythm gets altered, and in extreme cases broken, by perturbations.
  - Chaos signifies loss of rhythm.
- Continual improvement implies simplification or repeated application of incremental output or improvement in efficiency; however, this does not necessarily mean only an incremental impact.
- Re-engineering relates to process and workflow redesign.
  - The first step is to remove any wait or hands-off time, usually via automation.

- Second, is to attack superfluous and inefficient iterations to make 'hands-on' time more efficient.
- Third, all repetitive tasks themselves should be automated (e.g., via software bots).
- Innovation means identifying novel and new ways.
- Innovation can be achieved by breaking free from or overcoming time think and space think.

Chapter 8

Driving Business Transformation

The Cycle of Simplification and Re-creation

Transformation refers to an irreversible change into something different or barely recognizable. The *Oxford Dictionary* defines transformation as "a marked change in form, nature or appearance." Therefore, transformation can be changes in the physical character, the emotional character or the intelligence character of an entity, with very little retained from its past.

In the evolutionary cycles of change, transformations:

- Occur when something has died or is dying – symbolically or otherwise – to be born again as something new and different. It is not necessary that only living things need to die but it could even be death of inertia, dogmatism, cynicism or penury.
- Deliver a very large-scale impact.
- Are initiated in response to environment changes, or, within the DNA of the organism.
- Need a catalyst, huge energy and nutrients to support the change

145

- ▪ Cause large-scale changes in characteristics, whether physical, emotional or intellectual.
- ▪ Are irreversible, and
- ▪ Catalyze step changes accompanied by a degree of pain but followed by a sustained period of tranquility and stability.

On the STA strategy triangles chart, *transformation signifies death followed by creation*; or in short *end-of-life followed by rebirth*. It is critical that both states have occurred in sequence to qualify for transformation. The epigenetic mechanism that a business uses during the contraction phase is continual improvement. When such an activity ceases, the business degrades slowly; this portends the demise of the business. The business is now either ready to transform or become extinct.

Transformations occur in two forms – the inter-lifecycle transformations and the intra-lifecycle transformations. Whenever participating objects undergo transformation themselves, they reflect instances of intra-lifecycle transformations or change within their own lives. When they are the cause of the transformations in the environment, they have catalyzed inter-lifecycle transformation or have transformed others.

Table 8.1 illustrates instances of intra-lifecycle transformations.

8.1 Business Transformations – Types and Impact

There are two types of transformations – generative and disruptive.

- ▪ *Generative* transformations are like nature's divergent genetic re-engineering mechanism (e.g., the evolution of humans from primates). First, the transformation

Table 8.1 Transformations – Types, Causes, Impact and Examples

Cause of Impact		Transformation type (Impact)	
		Generative	*Disruptive*
Participants	*Living*		
	Non-living	Moore's Law, Internet, cellular technology, human machine partnership, quantum computing	Robots, technology – blockchain, 3D printer, open source hardware
Environmental Ecosystem	*Virtual*	The European Union, micro-lending, Aadhaar platform in India	Platforms, eCommerce marketplaces
	Real	Dubai, Las Vegas, public sector of Singapore	Hydroelectric dams, nuclear reactors

is spectacular, whether in a species, an operating environment, or the surroundings; second, when initiated they have the tendency to continuously spawn into something new along multiple threads – like an amoeba expanding in all its edges, albeit over time. Its modus of impact is strengthening the stronger and the naturally selected species without necessarily exterminating its ancestral kind (e.g., both man and primates coexist, and each has evolved at its own pace over time). Generative transformations have little negative impact on the majority of the population within the environment. On the contrary, it has an extremely positive impact for most species within that environment. Hence, generative transformations are value-accretive for all and are like the first-order lever that amplifies a small effort into a large force capable of moving big objects.

■ *Disruptive* transformations are equivalent to nature's mass extinctions and although not sudden and occurs over time, they creep up from behind, with all warnings of their impending approach getting missed or getting ignored. Disruptive transformations almost pervasively, impact negatively, majority of the population within the habitat. Few survive in such changed relief of the environmental ecosystem. Those left behind need to adapt to the new environment unleased post the event as there is a complete breakdown of all previous assumptions. However, the new world is always better, provided inertia is discarded and the new order of the world is quickly recognized and adopted.

One fact that singularly differentiates between the two types of transformations is that the disruptive transformations impose a rethink in the organizational strategy of the impacted largely by the fear of being out-maneuvered, while generative transformations are readily accepted due the virtues of its adoption and promise of continued redemption.

Transformations impact and are impacted by two broad entities – environmental-ecosystems and participating objects.

- Environmental-ecosystems are those that can be *real* or *virtual* environments and networks. The real environments refer to habitats on the earth like cities and villages but are truly extendible to anything within the cosmos; the virtual environmental ecosystems are man-made environments like economic markets, co-operatives and trading blocs.
- Participants are either *living* beings or *non-living* objects. These are entities that are either impacted by or impact the environmental ecosystems.
    - Non-living objects are those like robots and technology. Non-living objects could also refer to intelligent machines which would include smart vehicles and smart homes.
    - Living participants are natural living organisms in the universe, including man. In addition, based on Hall's exemplary research, both companies and cities behave like living beings. Companies are remarkably akin to natural living beings – they are born, they evolve and finally, they die; cities never die. Hence, companies have been classified as living participating objects while cities as real environmental ecosystems above.

8.2 Generative Transformations

Generative transformations are always additive in nature. They are like connector-extensions that provide a seemingly seamless link from the act of dissolution of the old to the act of creation of the revolutionary new. The dissolution (i.e., the trigger for any generative transformation), is akin to a long-distance runner 'hitting the wall' – with his body completely devoid of glycogens and no energy to go forward. The runner takes a short breather followed by ingesting carbohydrates for 'extending the run.' So are generative transformations.

Generative transformation represents:

■ A connector or an extension that breathes a new life into a business, technology or an event that is headed towards a confirmed end-of-life condition.
■ Renewal or a manifestation in a new form or state.
■ Long drawn and sustained effort.
■ Large-scale, positive impact, post the transformation event.
■ Low or no negative impact for the larger environment.
■ The inherent capability of self-organizing into multiple threads, each charting its own path of transformation.

This section presents several examples of generative transformations; in all the cases the business or the entity was confronted with a definite loss of momentum due to an impending end-of-life event or hitting-the-wall conditions. This occurs when peak performance has been achieved and without a change in strategy or in assumptions, the business or the technology will hit-the-wall and get into a stall. It can also happen when a natural disability, helplessness or a limiting environment frustrates one into sub-par performance. Generative transformations can be viewed as a virtuous cycle of repeated evolutions, fueled by positive feedback from each such iteration, and constantly becoming better from the previous best. One of the best examples cited is by Professor Govindarajan, who explains the evolution of high-jumping styles in the Olympics. Each time the records plateaued the jumpers adopted a new style of jumping – from scissors to western-roll to straddle to Fosbury flop – for breaching the previous record. This is a great example of generative transformation because each transformation effort created a connector-extension from where the previous method 'hit-the-wall' or reached the peak record. However, this is also an example of a deeply stalled generative-transformation. The Fosbury flop was an innovation of the late 1960s and nothing new has emerged since then.

The cycle of generative transformation is charted on the following strategy triangles diagram (Figure 8.1). The innermost triangle is the *triangle of dissolution* or the 'wall' where the end-of-life event awaits the business or the entity. This is the trigger for a generative transformation to begin. The middle triangle is the *triangle of evolution* or sustaining innovation. This is the usual expansion phase for any innovation. The

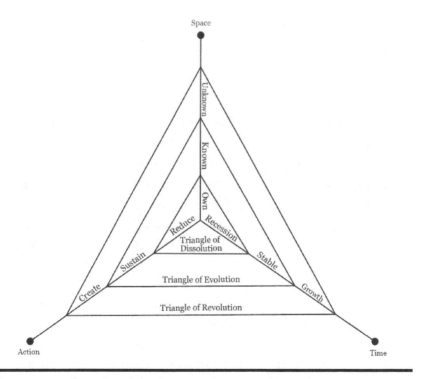

Figure 8.1   The Triangles of Generative Transformations

outermost triangle is the *triangle of revolution* or the strategy triangle where the generative transformation is initiated, after the trigger comes from the triangle of dissolution and the fear of tomorrow. A participant who goes through multiple cycles of dissolution and revolution, traverses through the virtuous and accretive cycles of generative transformations, as they are tied to unbounded positive feedback.

8.2.1 Generative Transformation Unleashed by Living Beings

There are innumerable examples of human transformation that owe their genesis to human gratitude or the will to make a difference to others. There are many such examples in the business too. What makes it even more amazing is that it is not only the rich and the abundant that become galvanized to tread on this path but even very ordinary mortals. Likewise, it has been the corporations sometimes that have catalyzed such transformations, and at other times, their employees.

*

It was towards the end of 2004 when Delta Airlines filed for Chapter 11 bankruptcy – the end of an era. Ridden with debt, with the rising cost of fuel, over-populated workforce, poor-employee relations, inefficient operations, and coming out of the bankruptcy in 2007, Delta management decided to transform itself. It did so and as of today it is one of the largest airlines in the world, recently awarded with the 'Airline of the Year' award and is a completely new being, a pale shadow of which existed in the early 2000s.

Innovation or transformations were not new to Delta. Delta was the first airline to introduce the hub-and-spoke system. However, this transformation was not simple and the CEO, Richard Anderson, decided to follow a distinctly untrodden path. Employees became part of a significant 15% stock ownership plan and a 10% profit-sharing program; the airlines expanded its geographical reach by partnering with five foreign airlines and merging with Northwest Airlines. One of the most unconventional moves was to acquire an oil refinery and integrate vertically with crude suppliers to procure fuel cheaper than what the market offered, as well as become insulated from large price swings. The airlines overhauled its fleet by reducing smaller aircrafts, changed the frequent flier program to dollars spent instead of miles travelled and expanded into several ancillary verticals. Anderson in an article in the *Harvard Business Review* in 2014 claimed that other than the hard work and tireless efforts of the people, it was 'the Delta culture' that allowed them to bring innovation back to them, something that they were once known for. But the real story had begun many years ago.

*

'The Spirit of Delta' was an exceptionally powerful transformation of Delta in 1983 – only it was not the corporation but the employees of Delta who catalyzed the transformation – a rare case of generative transformation triggered due to the deep gratitude of the employees. Troubled by the aftershocks of the air traffic controllers' strike, high fuel prices and a weak economy, for the first time in the previous 25 years, Delta, otherwise a hugely profitable company, had posted a substantial loss. Delta was not alone as all its peers too had suffered a similar fate – nearly forty thousand employees from other airlines had lost their jobs. Contrary to the actions of its peers and in line with its own 'Delta culture,' Delta gave an 8.5% average pay rise to its employees. Overwhelmed by this move, the employees decided to demonstrate their gratitude by giving 'wings' to their expression. They decided to buy Delta their first Boeing 767 as a thank-you gift! Galvanizing momentum over an intense three-month period, they succeeded in collecting over 77% of the 30 million dollars needed to buy the plane.

On the morning of December 15, over seven thousand employees, their friends and a large contingent of international media gathered to see the employee representatives deliver the sparkling gift to the senior management of Delta – and on the jet was inscribed, "The Spirit of Delta." The 'spirit' flew as the flag of Delta culture and camaraderie for over 23 years. It journeyed back home on May 7, 2006 to proudly retire and rest at the Delta Museum, Historic Hangar 2.

8.2.2 Generative Transformation Activated by Non-living Objects

It has been widely researched and well established that *networks* and *network effect* create immense value – both socially as well as commercially. While networks connotes 'an interconnection of people or devices that can exchange information,' the network effect refers to the law of increasing returns or the additional exponential value created as the network grows. W.Brian Arthur, a key proponent of increasing returns, articulated that the knowledge industries are mostly led by this phenomenon as they not only depend upon optimization but also adaptation, which means watching for next wave and taking advantage of it.

Today with the advent of technology, networks and network effects are assuming a central role in the lives of the people as the world rapidly shrinks into a connected planet through digital transformation. However, the three prime movers that have been the force accelerating the digital world are Moore's law, the Internet and cellular technology.

Gordon Moore, the founder of Intel, projected that every 24 months the power of the chip doubles and the price halves. This was further revised by David House, his CEO, with the power of hardware doubling every 18 months and the cost being halved. Although originally enumerated nearly 50 years ago, the law still seems to be holding true, although not likely for too long. This is a testimony to the pace of continuous innovation in chip design that promises in advance delivering 2× computing power at lower price and form factors indefinitely – till it finally breaks down. What this pace of hardware innovation has engineered close on its toes, is an ever-hungry pace of software innovation for doing more complex work in much larger domains. Ultimately, it has made power computing ubiquitous, cheap and accessible to all and is probably the first successful bridge that has removed the divide between the haves and the have-nots in the most resounding inclusion worldwide. In fact, developing and under developed nations are the biggest consumers of both basic or feature phones and smart phones – a direct link to information access and growing prosperity.

The Internet was an US Department of Defense funded project for creating a fault tolerant network of interconnected computer systems that could communicate in a secure form. It was academia that took advantage of this experiment before the commercialization of the Internet began. Today, the Internet is pervasive and akin to oxygen while Internet freedom is akin to democracy. The combination of Moore's law and the Internet has given rise to successful deployment of the cloud, IaaS, SaaS and PaaS, which means that small start-ups and companies do not need an expensive IT infrastructure and systems or personnel to run it, a boon to entrepreneurial impetus. Infrastructure and software are available metered on a tap.

Finally, cellular technology fixed the last mile problem. The high-speed Internet was a wired technology initially, became wireless within buildings to avoid expensive internal wiring, and, finally, was delivered on cellular devices on the move. The initial cellular technologies could deliver only a few kilobits per second of browsing and access speeds; the current 5G can go as high as one gigabit per second. This makes powerful apps on smartphone and tablets, which are easier to build and deploy, accessible to millions of users worldwide. Moore's law, the Internet and cellular technology are in the state of maturity. All three work in tandem and are hidden in the background now.

The *human-machine continuum* undoubtedly is the next step in generative transformation. The lazy human being will outsource any task it can to the machine, but he needs to be careful as to how much intelligence he wants to transfer to his non-living alter-ego. The human–machine continuum mimics the time–space dimension where the underlying strategy is to match strengths with opportunities. This defines a division of labor where clear handovers between the human and the machine exists to maximize human output. However, the continuum will allow the machine to take over from the human being in some predefined areas when the human being fails, like David Hasselhoff's car 'KITT' in the television series *Knight Rider* with an easily bruised ego but designed to preserve its occupant under all conditions.

The initial experiments began with human–machine interactions, which were to primarily make the interface between human and the machines with their software more intuitive and user-experience driven. The human–machine coordination and cooperation are centered more around machine learning and predisposition towards cooperation. The current stage of the research is focused on human–machine partnerships – which will allow machines to take decisions without bias and emotions in conjunction with human control and judgement. With Moore's law still going strong and the computing power of the chip that could soon become frighteningly fast, machines do have the capability of overtaking the human brain, but only in the area we humans want. However, there may be a twist to this story.

*

There are two strong reasons why Moore's law may reach its limits soon.

- The first is the miniaturization of the chips will reach atomic levels. The chips are made of transistors, which act as electrical switches (i.e., allow or disallow the passage of electrons). But if miniaturization reaches the size of the electron itself, then how can an electron pass through it! This means that quantum physics will come into play.
- Second, it is the economics rather than the physics alone that will cause a deeper bottleneck. According to the last International Technology Roadmap for Semiconductors (ITRS), released in 2016, the global computing infrastructure is already hogging a significant share of the world's power. The ITRS forecasts that by 2040 computing will need more electricity than what the world can itself produce.

With a proliferation of Internet of Things devices, big data and healthcare applications projected to exponentially increase, both above limitations will inhibit any large-scale and meaningful deployments. However, both these major edge limitations have spurred enormous research, predicated primarily on nanotechnology and quantum physics. The single electron transistor (SET) is an experimental technology in this direction. The key advantages are very low power consumption, and, a very high device integration that achieves large circuits in small spaces. The European Union has already funded a project that is looking at feasibility of mass manufacturing of SET devices at room temperatures. But the larger research is in the *quantum computing* area.

The quantum computing research has been pursued from the mid-1980s. Quantum physics essentially governs the world of the very small and elementary particles (like electrons, protons and neutrons) can persist in two or more states at once (i.e., can exist as a wave and a particle). This can be used to harness the processing unit of a quantum computer. A computer essentially performs two functions – stores 0s and 1s in simple switches and uses logical gates to perform mathematical and logical functions. The processor is sequential as it fetches and executes one instruction at a time. A small degree of parallelism in processing can be achieved by writing a parallel program and orchestrating all the threads on multiple processors running concurrently.

The quantum computing researchers are translating the same mechanism of storing bits and manipulating them on subatomic particles. An electron, for example, can spin either up or down on its axis, and therein lies the mechanism of representing a 1 or a 0 respectively. We call this, a qubit. Going beyond, it is possible to even have an in-between condition 75% up and 25% down. This is called *superposition* of spin states. The superposition of spin states in an electron allows it to mimic digital gate operations. Lov Grover, in his lucid paper, takes the example of a single molecule of $CHCl_3$ (chloroform) and by using just its carbon and the hydrogen atoms and changing their spin direction, shows how a controlled-NOT gate can be implemented – which can reverse engineer inputs from a given output. It is important to note that any quantum operation changes all states directly at once *in parallel*. Thus, if there are 2 qubits possible like in the example above, 2^2 or 4 states are simultaneously possible. If a larger molecule was to be taken which could represent x qubits, then 2^x states become possible. Grover quotes the example of a million, unordered names and telephone number; it would take a 20 qubits quantum machine to simultaneously represent the entire dataset in one single shot and any name or telephone search would be just one cycle! In a conventional computer it would be between 500,000 and 999,999 searches. This also means that today's password encryption methods, however secure, will get broken with equal ease.

Michael Nielsen, a pioneer and an eminent researcher in the study of quantum computing, on observing that adding a qubit doubles the information needed to define the quantum computer, created a quantum analogue of Moore's law: "to keep pace with conventional computers, quantum computers need only add single qubit every two years." As of going to the press, IBM has just unveiled a 53-qubit cloud-based quantum machine that will be available to the public! Google is rumored to have a 72-qubit device but it is available only for their internal use. The quantum supremacy heat is on!

8.2.3 Generative Transformation Activated by Virtual Environmental Ecosystem

Three hugely successful experiments that have unarguably transformed the lives of a large population are the formation of the European Union, Bangladesh's micro lending and India's Aadhaar. There are many others too but we will restrict to these three only. The EU website clearly defines what it is and what it is not. The EU is neither a federal arrangement like the US as each of the EU member states is sovereign; nor is it an intergovernmental organization like the United Nations, as the member states do pool their sovereignty – in the areas where it makes sense to do so, thereby deriving greater collective strength and influence. The EU has built a single market based on four pillars, i.e., with people, goods, services and capital moving freely through the 28 member states. They also have a common currency making transactions far more efficient than if native currency conversions were to take place between the nations. The impact can be easily ascertained by comparing the improved relative prosperity of newer EU states like Estonia, Latvia and Lithuania versus its other Soviet Federal counterparts, which broke away from the USSR at the same point in time as the formers but are way behind in terms of prosperity, containment of local strife and governance.

*

The Grameen Foundation website highlights some poignant and stark realities – 70% of the world's poorest people are farmers; women who make the bulk of the food are locked out from access to markets, credit, land ownership and training; more than 2 billion people globally have no access to financial services. The Grameen founder and Nobel Laureate, Professor Muhammad Yunus, created a micro lending bank for the poor who neither had any credit or banking history, nor did they have any collateral to pledge against their loans. These were poor farmers who needed money to grow crops and sustain themselves for the entire period of cultivation before the produce could be harvested and sold. Yunus extended very small loans or provided micro-finance to such borrowers on trust and mutual respect who otherwise would have to borrow from loan sharks. Yunus' impact on the poor not only in Bangladesh but across many other countries in the world has been well documented by the World Bank and many other agencies. The bank has had a 99% recovery and has disbursed, collateral free, US$24 billion in micro-credit to around 9 million borrowers. They also make normal banking profits!

*

Governments are most capable of thinking in terms of scale but not very efficient in implementing that vision and creating the impact in a short period. However, the story of Aadhaar is different.

The Indian constitution is unique in its approach. When India achieved its independence the financial condition of the country was in tatters. The framers of the Indian constitution knew very well that with such a poor state of economy, issues like right to education, right to livelihood, right to medical support, etc., would not have been sustainable. Hence, they not only created fundamental rights, something that every citizen in the democratic republic is guaranteed by the courts, but also created the 'directive principles,' which the State and central governments should strive to achieve whenever the time was ripe in future.

Governments have relied upon bureaucracy, self-governing bodies and a chain of financial institutions to distribute subsidy and relief to the needy. However, the channel has been very porous, as inefficiency and graft have caused large-scale diversion of funds. The Indian government embarked upon an ambitious plan of establishing biometric identity of all the citizens of India with Aadhaar, which when translated from Hindi means 'the basis of one's existence.' It took the private–public–community partnership to create this highly technologically advanced infrastructure and onboard close to one billion people issuing each one a unique identity as a bona-fide citizen of India. Subsidy is no longer provided on the selling price to the producers – everyone buys at the full price. All subsidy is now routed directly to the recipient's bank account linked to Aadhaar, thereby also creating a trail of the transaction. Not everything is perfect though, and we in India have a long way to go in this journey, but this effort surpasses the litmus test of a true transformation on all three major counts – in its scale, its impact and the fact that something needs to die or is dying, which is poverty and graft.

It is important to note that in each of these cases the transformation is not finished yet. The impact of the good will continue to multiply and spawn into other acts.

8.2.4 Generative Transformation of Real Environmental Ecosystem

The global population in 1951 was 2.7 billion with 30% of the people living in urban centers. In 2018, the corresponding statistics were 7.6 billion with 55% of the people living in urban centers. The UN projection for 2050 is a global population of about 9.3 billion with 68% living in urban centers. These huge urban migrations will need to be concomitant with sustainable development of economic, social and environmental scopes such that the benefits of urbanization are shared by all. It will be India, China and Nigeria that will account for 35% of the growth in urban population between 2018 and 2050, according to the UN report, with India at 416 million, China at 255 million and Nigeria at 189 million. These will mandatorily need to be scripted as a generative real ecosystem and environment transformation; failure to do this will be no less than a disaster.

*

For a city to thrive and be highly 'livable' it must score highly both on infrastructural and socio-economic elements. In developed countries this is quite true. In most neo-developed countries, the former has usually preceded the latter (e.g., Singapore, Dubai, Hongkong), while in most developing countries it is socio-economic growth that has spurred infrastructure growth (e.g., Bangalore and Manila). Thus, the difference is one where the vision of creating a global city that attracts the right ingredients to spur growth, precedes an accidental economic activity like software development or financial services that helps to generate enough revenue for the municipal corporations to build the infrastructure but at a lag with growth. However, the shortage of fiscal resources globally is forcing city authorities to make better use of their existing resources and capacities. This is where smart cities are coming in.

*

The generative transformation of any city begins with changing the skyline of the city and hence transforming the sub-linear correlated infrastructural elements. Modern architecture, well planned amenities, operating utilities around the clock, careful ecological balance and a monitored, supportive industry that is encouraged to behave responsibly, is the core theme of any such transformation. Simultaneously, the levers of unbounded growth trigger step-increments in socio-economic elements as they correlate super-linearly with an increase in size of the city, as discussed earlier. However, since every generative transformation also brings with itself unavoidable downsides as these get equally over-accentuated like their positive counterparts, these need to be contained. Crime, accidents, waste, vehicle pollution, traffic gridlocks or misuse of natural resources are a few such examples that also increase with growth and need to be tackled.

The use of technology to build smart cities are the next phase of generative city transformation. The objectives remain the same – driving more out of the existing resources and capacities in the wake of exponentially increasing urban population. The pervasive use of sensors in addition to the enormous computing power and networks available, are helping cities become smarter by extending the life of aged assets, continuously monitoring critical environmental parameters, monitoring activities like traffic, events and protests or responding to and preventing crime-in-progress through centralized command and control centers. Of course, there is much more to come.

8.3 Disruptive Transformations

Disruptive transformations are a near-exact opposite of generative transformations. The genesis of disruptive transformations is deeply rooted in the need for applying significant *impulse* to achieve *scale*. An impulse signifies a very large force applied for a very short period. This is true for most start-ups since they have money in short supply and need to deliver a minimum viable product as fast as possible to the market. This is equally true for large organizations racing to achieve a breakthrough in their research projects (e.g., in molecular or drug research); however, the leeway for them is larger due to their staying power. This is one of the key reasons why start-ups disrupt much more than established players. The start-ups also achieve their impulse by dilutions at very high valuations, thereby getting access to inordinate amounts of funds that an established organization may not be able to allocate, even if they had reserves, because of minimum returns that the ordinary shareholders would hold them to from regular operations.

Earlier in Section 3.3, we studied that on the time–action dimension, the most likely disruptors are either the demand side participants or participants that display attitudinal economics – the new economy participants. Since they largely rely on impulse, they can also be referred to as the *impulse participants*. However, the attitudinal participants could deliver another critical large impact – they can convert disruptive transformation into the more powerful and more democratic generative transformations, and this will be seen soon.

Disruptive transformations are usually:

■ A cause of mass-extinction of competing businesses
■ A cheaper, efficient, easier or a more elegant alternative to the current way of delivering value – via product or service. They are accompanied by a significant negative side-impact to a large section of competing participants.
■ Impulse driven, where the disruptor is focused on a narrow sub-segment, the overlooked or lower end of the customers.
■ A result of an externally initiated stimulus, generally under radar or innocuous looking, with the disruptor not even pre-gauging the extent of disruption that the change can trigger.

- When fully mature, triggers an end-of-life for the current way of conducting business or application of technology.
- Accompanied by systematic breakdown of all core assumptions
- Where the market or the technology needs time to recalibrate to the new and disruptive methods. Any adoption is out of the fear of being outmaneuvered or to dip your toes to be at least in the periphery of the game.

Usually a participant unleashes an innovation to solve a specific unfulfilled customer need, an industry problem or simply doing an existing task more efficiently or elegantly. The innovation either unwittingly disrupts the contemporary way of doing things (e.g., Google and Amazon), or it can be applied to a very different use-case in a very different industry thereby unintentionally threatening disruption in that industry (e.g., blockchain technology and 3D printers). *The disruptive transformations are thus clear instances of strategy-encirclements.*

The cycle of disruptive transformation is charted on the strategy-encirclements diagram (Figure 8.2). The outermost circle is the *circle of revolution* or the strategy encirclement where the destructive transformation gets triggered. Often, the trigger is underrated and non-threatening to most established players in the similar competitive space. The middle circle or the *circle of evolution* is the innovation–expansion phase where the initiating participant is deeply engaged in. This phase may even trigger a small contagion of diverse players within the competitive space. The innermost circle is the *circle of dissolution* or the 'entrapment' where the end-of-life event awaits the business entity due to the negative impact of the innovation unleashed in the outermost encirclement. Thus, disruptive transformations, are like currents that move outside-in on the action axis of the STA diagrams, quite unlike

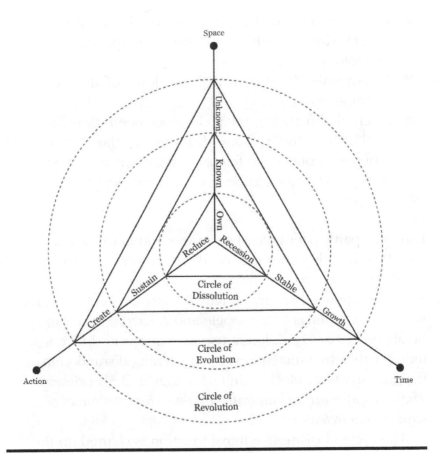

Figure 8.2 Disruptive Transformations Encirclements

generative transformations, which have an inside-out direction of travel like the eruption of a volcano. Most affected players get grievously affected due to ignorance, lack of agility and exhibiting the 'too-little-too-late' syndrome. Group think, space think, and time think exacerbate the situation further and the strategies to counter the ill-effects were elaborated in earlier sections.

8.3.1 Disruptive Transformations Unleashed by Living Beings

Science reached a tipping point towards the end of nineteenth century. The digital technology movement seems to be reaching its tipping point now. It threatens to disrupt every industry. The digital disruptors of today are no longer constrained by the speed of thinking or the speed of simultaneous experimentation with radically different approaches. Nor are they hindered by the unavailability of an out-of-the-box, large-scale, tested solution. Despite this, the new-age competitors are driving scale at a pace that the classical old economy companies are not used to. Instead of relying on the traditional methods of trying to look for a pattern among the traditional winners, the disruptors launch multiple experiments to solve the problem within multiple sub-dimensions. Failures don't daunt them, and the nimbleness and mindset improve the speed of response and consequently the odds of success hugely in their favor.

The creation of cloud services and, with them, the service mesh and the micro services, is not credited to traditional software companies; this is also not a standalone example. Many core technologies of today like big data, data analytics and deep machine learning have become formidable technologies because of the impulse participants needing more incisive insights from the large masses of data that they were collecting. The network economy was thus rapidly disrupting the traditional technology boundaries and more value was being generated by collaboration outside of the internal network and technology suppliers.

Cloud services were conceived as a public utility way back in the 1960s. However, it was Amazon who first offered the cloud commercially as an infrastructure-as-a-service with the launch of AWS, the Amazon Web Services, in 2002. Amazon upped this with the release of EC2, elastic compute cloud, in 2006, and, it was Google, another non-traditional technology company, which were the next to release their cloud services in 2008. However, it was only in 2010 when the first large commercial software company, Microsoft, released its version of the cloud – Microsoft Azure. This was followed by the IBM Smart Cloud in 2011 and Oracle Cloud in 2012 – exactly a decade after Amazon had first released it. It is not difficult to deduce what triggered this 'contagion' and why the releases were so close to each other for the commercial software companies.

Cloud services, so ubiquitous today and a key reason for the pervasive proliferation of start-ups, came into Gartner's prime view only in 2008. Not hindered by the fact that a commercial software company had not yet announced a cloud offering, or that the futurists were yet to describe the full leverage of the cloud, Netflix in 2008 had already decided to adopt it. Netflix took eight years to move to the cloud but to utilize the elasticity of the cloud as well as improve the streaming quality they innovated several technologies that were non-existent before (e.g., the micro services and istio service mesh), and freely shared with the computing world through open source. Folklore says that Netflix hogs nearly one-third of America's total bandwidth during prime time. With such a scale of operations for Amazon and Netflix, when even the world was just warming up to the art of possible from the cloud, the only viable option was to drive innovation. The traditional software companies collaborated only as coalition partners. The last large-scale entrant into the cloud is Alibaba, which followed Amazon's path to build its cloud business. They are on an overdrive now.

So how do the traditional companies and impulse organizations differ? In addition to the disruptor characteristics stated in the Section 3.3 on *consumer–producer relationships*, there are two others worthy of a special mention here as these are crucial essentials for disruptive transformations. The first is the *speed of response matrix* and the second is the use of *technology as an enabler versus its use as a differentiator.*

Table 8.2 below plots the core competitive advantages of legacy firms versus impulse organizations. While the former primarily see technology as a differentiator (e.g., an ERP product is positioned being better vis-à-vis its competitors on the basis of a differentiated feature list), the latter sees it mostly as a key enabler for customer experience. The impulse business makes extremely effective use of technology to enable them to drive focused differentiation, i.e., customer data analysis, accurate insight on customers' habits and needs, recommendation algorithm, content curation and continuous novelty to make unobvious sense from it.

The impulse business also looks at exponential scaling as a deeply differentiating strategy and puts a lot of effort in global customer acquisition. The legacy business, on the other hand, looks at linear or super-linear scaling strategies and not generally exponential scaling – growth rates in most business plans will bear testimony to this fact, and relies upon the

Table 8.2 Competitive Advantages – Scale and Technology

		Business Type	
		Legacy (supply side business)	Impulse (Demand side and attitudinal business)
Competitive Advantage	Technology	Differentiator	Enabler and mostly shareable
	Scale	Meticulously planned against best-in-class global benchmarks or patterns	"Build the plane after you jump". At a scale usually 10× and not achieved before

supply chain to drive customer acquisition. There are some departures from the norm like Reliance Jio in India, which has adopted an impulse strategy for scaling; but the upfront resources and investments needed in such cases are equally humungous.

The following 2 × 2 table (Table 8.3) depicts the customer response matrix for a legacy firm and an impulse organization. While the legacy organizations respond to customer issues mostly based their service level obligations, in the impulse business the fix releases are so frequent that customers get new updates at very frequent intervals. When the outage is severe and sustained, like what Netflix faced due to exponential surge in customers, the solution(s) generated is likely a breakthrough, because of the uniqueness at a level of scale not touched before. In legacy software industries a workaround is shipped first followed by a long-term fix over time. In industries like the automotive industry, the vehicle needs to come to the service center

Table 8.3   Legacy vs. Impulse – Customer Response Matrix

		Business Type	
		Legacy scale (supply side business)	*Impulse scale (demand side and attitudinal business)*
Customer Impact	*Severe*	Workaround first and then planned fixes	Breakthrough fix
	Business – normal	Time graded fix	Daily fix release

and be evaluated before any warranty or free-of-cost service is processed. Rarely are the solutions dramatic enough to generate a breakthrough in approach.

8.3.2 Disruptive Transformations Activated by Non-living Objects

Jack Ma once observed, "Over the past twenty years, we have turned people into machines. In the future, we will turn machines into human beings." This captured both his dismay and his hope in a single line.

Over the past 20 years, one has seen the rules of business change ruthlessly. The neo-business environment has increasingly made it difficult for the traditional businesses. It, however, does not mean that the traditional business formats will cease to exist; it only signifies that these businesses will rapidly cease to be the benchmarks representing the best.

One must be reminded that disruption occurs when the stranglehold of the powerful becomes insidiously weakened by forces outside of their control, rendering them irrelevant over time. Will machines become smarter than humans or will this remain true only in the realm of science fiction movies? Earlier we cited an example of Deep Knowledge Ventures that has a robot on its board with full voting rights and how it has helped the firm to be successful in a highly volatile environment. Few though believe, non-withstanding Asimov's 'Three Laws of Robotics,' that robots will become smart enough to colonialize humans in the distant future – when they will achieve singularity. DeepMind, a UK-based AI company is working on Advanced General Intelligence (AGI), where machines like human beings will be able to learn multiple skills and deploy previously learned knowledge in learning new skills. Machine learning today is applicable for teaching very narrow and singly focused tasks like for example recommendation engines. If the task changes (e.g., recommending a hotel to a traveler versus a restaurant), the machine needs to be taught afresh as significantly different inputs are needed. Futurologist Dr Ian Pearson goes a step further and predicts the population of robots will outnumber the human population in not so distant a future. Today a robot can build its own factory. However, the general view is that human beings will not be entirely substituted by robots, but future intelligent companies will be a combination of 'smart machines with smart people.'

Robots are helping at many places especially in tackling the plight of humans where a lot of patience and empathy is needed. Socially interactive robots that can adopt multiple therapeutic roles for treating children with autism have been successfully experimented with, achieving positive results. Robots are now being used even for taking care of the elderly. In countries like Japan where the elderly population is on the rise and caregivers on the decline, such robots seem to be fast becoming their only option, despite a strong debate whether dying in the hands of robots, possibly in the absence of their family or even human nurses, is the unmistakable direction humanity is moving towards. Robots, without any remorse, will weed away mediocre workers, nurses, managers and even board-members of the future!

Chuck Hull, the inventor of 3D printer or Stereolithography, was researching ways to create quick prototypes from computer designs when he found a method of using UV light on photopolymers that turned them from liquids to solids instantly. From the first 3D prints in 1986 when the parts printed were brittle and distorted due to warpage, the chemistry has vastly improved and its applications vastly proliferated. Obvious areas like manufacturing, maritime, construction, education, prosthetics and printing of shoes have been successful targets, but even unobvious areas like medical imaging and bioprinting of human body parts, clothing and food are under investigation. Today the research is focused towards improving the speed of printing and volume of output (although this can be achieved via a factory of 3D printers) besides printing different types of materials. What began with a simple prototyping need is now transforming into an intelligent, generic mass-customization factory of tomorrow, which can print virtually anything from parts to apparels or from even food to houses, possibly in the same factory at lower cost, time and higher quality. This will likely disrupt many traditional industries. For starters, it would threaten the stranglehold of high-volume manufacturing giants globally, especially those in Asia. The disruption also threatens mankind's existence even further. Guns can be 3D printed now thus giving easy and unwanted access to criminals. Spurious replicas can propel mass-scale infringement of IPs – the exact opposite of what inhouse local prototyping was intended at. Even potential printing of hallucinogenic drugs could make drugs available without any physical movement or smuggling effort. Besides this, 3D printing is a high energy consumption device, which will plague the already stressed supply, until, of course, energy ultimately becomes free when man will finally have learned to harness it from abundant supply from the sun, wind and tides.

*

Disruptions seem to be rampaging though many stable boundaries. On a lighter note, Uzupis, a small neighborhood in Vilnius, the capital of Lithuania, was declared an independent micronation, on April 1, 1997, by a group of artists via a benign declaration with its chief pursuit being only artistic. Uzupis, though complete with its elected dignitaries, flag, anthem, constitution and currency, was never recognized by any other country. Micronations like Uzupis, are just a trivia for the world and have currency only for entertainment value as they are not backed by a true economy. A serious disruptive genie is in the making, which could change this – the blockchain revolution. Other than giving wings to this entertaining trivia, this serious genie could tear down many other holy grails – a result of yet another innocuous action.

In 2008, someone with a pseudonym, Satoshi Nakamoto, released a white paper that threatens to disrupt the way banking, finance, government, democracy, and transacting on the Internet will function in future. But this wasn't the core intent of the paper. For reasons only known to Satoshi, he created a self-contained but a distributed environment where anybody could join and transact without a certifying authority validating the authenticity of the person transacting. The platform was designed in such a way that it could conclusively establish the ownership of the digital asset under sale as well as the ownership of the currency, which he termed bitcoin or cryptocurrency. Bitcoins were mined based on a puzzle and this proof of work was recorded to determine indisputably the owner of a unique bitcoin. Every transaction was recorded in a distributed ledger via blocks and each block had its own hash, a code generated using the data on the block and encryption passwords. This meant that if any data were to be changed in the block retrospectively, the hash would not match, and the block would be rendered 'corrupt' and sequenced out of the blockchain. Thus, Satoshi's system created a secure, indelible and transparent record of the transaction with a copy of the ledger available with all the participants.

Whether Satoshi wanted to create a self-contained game in a fictional fairy-tale village or planned to purposely bypass federal governments by creating his own crypto-currency, is unknown. However, his method was so elegant and applicability so pervasive that futurists and technologists took notice and a huge rush of use cases with previously accepted deficiencies surfaced with seemingly stunning resolutions. Examples included transaction costs of currency transfers at virtually no costs, unhindered transfer of monies across the boundaries of countries, direct buyer-to-seller interaction without any intermediary or a platform to shave off percentage points, as well as no requirement for annual auditing of accounts. Each of these promises to reduce the cost of transactions substantially and break down significant bastions of controls that powerful institutions like banks, insurance agencies, auditing firms and governments yield today. Issuing currency will no more be within the confines of governments, banks will cease to be the only means of establishing creditworthiness or confirming availability of funds, auditors will not be required any more to sign off audited books of accounts as the copy of distributed ledger with every participant would itself house the audited accounts, money laundering can now be tracked easily and so can the assets, and, finally, the participants themselves will become the ombudsman resolving their own financial discrepancies or conflicts. The potential is enormous and the blockchain technology is here to mass-disrupt and accelerate legacy mass-extinctions. Without doubt, delayed adoption, or at least, evaluation of impact, of this rapidly evolving technology, could expose organizations to a certain disruption. Governments will also probably bring in legislation in the near future to deal with this technology. Security hardening to ward off cyber-attacks will be the obvious direction of travel for this technology. Libra, bootstrapped by Facebook with several other commercial organizations, is an attempt in this direction. It is an open source blockchain code, for Libra coin, touted to be the future virtual global currency that can enable anyone who just has a smart phone.

8.3.3 Disruptive Transformations Activated within Real Ecosystems

Neighborhood communities are a key element in building reciprocal trust, increasing volunteering and bettering civic engagement. Communities are helpful even in community stabilization when it goes through a crisis. However, there is more to communities than just the above. Over the past 200 years many researchers have studied the impact of community on human lives, and from simple observational correlations to now advanced studies using big data, the impact seems to be far more than what we could have ever imagined. Today communities are no longer restricted by geographical or locality constraints. Internet has helped in extending these into large global, virtual communes and they are now playing highly expanded roles clearly evidenced by Twitter or Instagram, just as an example.

*

Democracy and communities are one of the biggest disruptors within the real space. They are also deeply interconnected. Democracy is a network of all people within a nation with assembly and self-representation rights. It has been a key disruptor of autocracy and communism across the ages; wherever the two have died, democracy was born, and both, the countries and the people, were transformed.

Alexis de Tocqueville, a French diplomat and a researcher, travelled to the United States of America in 1830–1831 to study their prisons. He realized that the fortunes of this soon-to-be-great nation rested entirely upon how differently they had interpreted and implemented democracy. The transformation from aristocracy to democracy seemed to be reluctant and slow within Europe, as the nobles were being forced to cede their power to the common man. France, for example, saw a revolution every 50 years, starting from the eleventh century, which was responsible for slow but continuous reduction of the gap between the noblemen and the common men. Thus, the rate of democratization was sluggish and tortuous. America, on the other hand, never had a monarchy or feudalism. Unlike the laws in France, like inheritance of land only by the oldest son, the equivalent law in the US firmly established the equality of inheritance and the law of equal division to all the children. This had a bolstering effect in reinforcing democracy. Land parcels dwindled and so did the power of land owners over the working class. Over a couple of generations, the parcels became smaller and the inheritors were dispositioned towards selling and moving to other places. This reduced the local clout of the so-called family of landlords.

Communities, a micro entity within a country, further check misuse of power; they are disruptors of nepotism and corruption in institutions dealing with public interfaces. John Keane, who traced the history of democracy and the stages of its evolution speaks of 'monitory democracy' as the current form of democracy. Monitory democracy represents a slew of measures through non-government and civic institutions like the civil liberty network in the US or election commission in India, that are formulated to keep in check unbridled power that elected governments, the executive or the judiciary can abuse. Thus, democracy has the impulse force that transformed the relationship between the people and those who ruled their land. One of the biggest beneficiaries of democracy has been the business community that enjoys free and unconstrained market forces.

There are some other examples of disruption in the real ecosystems too. For example, dams and nuclear power plants, although very beneficial when built, are both disruptive for the communities and destructive for the flora and fauna in the region. However, the discussion on disruption is to exemplify how the most unlikely detractors without resources rout the strong and the entrenched; not how the strong are able to disrupt the weak – that remains an act of helplessness faced with destruction.

8.3.4 *Disruptive Transformations in Virtual Environment Ecosystems*

Networks are important as networks strengthen communities, which in turn strengthen democracy. Since information is power, any medium that helps to disseminate information freely helps in giving power to the people and enforcing social equality. Networks disseminate data as well as knowledge. Thus, networks rapidly perpetuate democratization. The power of networks could be very sobering, and some countries opposed to such power have set up extensive infrastructure to monitor and suppress such a free flow.

Networks disrupt legacy businesses. Networks also extend real ecosystems like real communities into virtual communities. Thus, networks have the power of rapid expansion across defined borders, free and unrestrained access to information, and quick enrolment of new members. While communities are usually local with regional interests, networks could be global with communities with both local and global interests.

All platform businesses are network businesses. Platform businesses are aggregators and orchestrators. Both buyers and sellers are on the platform and can interchange their roles, which is why platforms can ensure better matches between the suppliers and the buyers. Networks and consequently platforms have democratized buying. High-end accessories are no more a realm of duty-free shops or high street shops in fashionable cities alone, and so is access to the latest in white goods, consumables, movies, clothing, games and the list goes on and on. Whether it is rural or the semi-urban, everyone has access to the same information and goods and services, across the globe, something that was difficult even ten years ago. The large platforms have even created communities of the netizens on their platforms with similar tastes, whether reading or travelling or food or even finer tastes like wines, theatre and fine arts.

However, there is a distinct risk. What the law of inheritance did to the aristocrats and the land lords – which is divide and break large tracts of lands into smaller pieces owned by more people and hence dissolved the power associated with it – the networks could do exactly the reverse, which is create mammoths with large virtual territories. Thus, what unbridled power is to democracy, large masses of customer behavioral data are to the networks. While networks help in democratization of consumer access to choices, going beyond the boundaries of villages, cities and even countries, the aggregation of such large tracts of virtual spaces does make them over-powerful. There have been intense debates around net-neutrality, ethical use of consumer data and responsibility that the network and platform owners need to display. *If media was the fourth estate, networks are fast becoming the fifth estate.* Congressional hearings of the CEOs of Facebook and Google show just the start of what is more to come.

8.4 Maximizing between Generative and Disruptive Transformations

Both generative and disruptive transformations are critical levers for an organization to reinvent itself continually, to invest in the 'products of the future' and to stay relevant. Organizations use the three atomic levers – improvement, re-engineering and innovation, either in standalone or in combination, to drive such transformations. But it is not necessary that organizations need to hunt only for disruptive transformations to strike it big. Generative transformations can be a bigger and easier bet with far lower levels of risk. However, the answer will become visible only when organizations can break out of the shackles of time-think. **Living Beings Can only Be Transformed – They Cannot Be Innovated.** All living beings, including organizations, can only be transformed and not innovated. If something never existed, it cannot be transformed. To qualify for a transformation the key question that needs to be ascertained is, "what is dying or being killed?" If the answer to this critical question is, "nothing," then the act does not qualify for transformation.

Spawning Continuous Evolution vs. Impulse impact. Generative transformations work on the principles of 'good-begets-good'; hence, they induce more downstream innovation within the ecosystem. This is like a tree with many branches and each branch can itself grow into more branches. The combination of Moore's law, the Internet and cellular telephony is probably a great example that has been quoted in the text earlier. From a simple need for communication and collaboration, our main trunk that was seeded about 60 years ago, it has now spread into many critical branches. Quantum computing, digital technologies (that themselves have multiple sub-branches – robotics, artificial intelligence, data analytics, Internet of Things, smart technologies, etc.) and sustainability (decoding environment changes, electricity generation from the waste) just to name a few. If the advancements in the first three had not taken place, the cascade of downstream transformations would have been impossible.

Disruptive transformations are equally important as they force sudden dramatic improvements and operate as impulse agents. Since the improvement effects are so dramatic, and the bias for change so immediate, it hits the incumbents with the force of a tsunami, the moment the transformation is mature enough to be adopted. Disruption by definition is singular within a segment; hence either the segment needs to be broken into multiple sub-segments or new segments need to be attacked to hunt for more disruptive transformation. One of the biggest prime movers that has catalyzed disruptive transformation is technology; it will continue to be so. But in the long term, it will always be breaking down all existing assumptions on which current organizations are predicating their differentiation and existence upon and imprisoned in the clasp of time think.

The multiplicative power of disruptive transformations: *disruptive transformation + attitudinal economics (as a catalyst) = generative transformation:* So far we have seen disruptive transformations akin to impulse driven alpha males, rampaging through stable environments. Can disruptive transformations trigger generative transformation, hence making them symbiotic? The answer is yes and the catalyst is attitudinal force. One prime example is that of the cloud infrastructure, a disruptive technology that has virtually converted the hardware vendors of large machines to mostly B2B players and caused a near shutdown for traditional data centers. What began as a need for Amazon to convert their unconsumed, excess space and compute power into a provision-on-demand service for their customer, Netflix, has today blossomed into a completely transformed ecosystem, the ubiquitous cloud. The cloud is not something that hardware vendors would ever have likely invested their research dollars into. This successful experiment between the two initiators has now attracted several attitudinal participants and commercial firms alike, and some of the earlier mentioned open source software and methods that are available today like istio, or the micro services architecture, spawned from here. From a place where data centers took 15 days to provision a service and had a minimum contract duration that ranged in multiples of years, to a point where infrastructure-as-a-service is available on tap and can be provisioned in minutes, is a big transformation. Platforms as a service, software as a service and now anything as a service have all spawned out of the same branch and are based on the core attitudinal thesis of consuming the idle – including unused hardware. In fact, the subscription-based model is one of the key reasons why start-ups have been the biggest disruptors. The cloud, which disrupted the hardware vendors and data centers of yesteryear, kickstarted a generative transformation that has changed the way software and services are getting delivered today. The cause is attitudinal forces.

There are many examples of such a conversion from disruptive to generative technology. 3D printing, democracy and social networks are just a few.

Triggers for generative and disruptive transformations: Generative transformations are initiated within the innermost triangle of dissolution or via an 'impending end of life' trigger. This is followed by the phase of selective adoption by multiple but selective groups via the triangle of evolution. Finally, contagion or mass acceptance is triggered via the triangle of revolution where the new solution is generally acceptable to all.

Disruptive transformations, on the other hand, are initiated via the outermost circle of revolution activated by the 'systematic breakdown of core assumptions' trigger. The phase of selective adoption is usually a stealth expansion where the specific disruptive solution is tested by select groups; this is when the solution has moved to the circle of dissolution phase. Finally, the contagion or the mass acceptance is triggered via the circle of evolution where the new solution is rapidly adopted, and the entrenched companies realize that they have been disrupted.

Choosing between generative or disruptive transformation? Generative investments are longer lasting and have more threads to follow. Hence, these are less risky to invest in as there is an end-of-life expected soon and a solution is necessary. Stable and large organizations thus prefer to adopt this. It is also a powerful strategy for nation governments or slow innovating companies to continue with an innovation agenda that is a minimum as prescribed by the strategy-triangle. The smaller companies, on the other hand, rely on impulse and hence adopt more disruptive strategies. Disruption is very specific. Sometimes the rate at which the organization is blitzscaling breaks down all its operational and

Table 8.4 Generative vs. Disruptive Transformations

Transformation Characteristics	Generative	Disruptive
Something, that must have died or is dying – symbolically or otherwise – to be born again and evolve into something else very different. It is not necessary that only living things need to die but it could even be death of inertia, dogmatism, cynicism or penury.	A connector or an extension that breathes new life into a business, technology or an event in a certain end-of-life condition.	A cheaper, efficient, easier or a more elegant alternative to the current way of delivering value (product or service). It is accompanied by a significant negative side-impact to a large section of competing participants, but usually over time.
Deliver a very large-scale impact.	A renewal or a manifestation in a new form or state. Usually long drawn and sustained.	Impulse driven, where the disruptor is focused on a narrow sub-segment, the overlooked or lower end of the customers.
Initiated in response to environment changes, or, within the DNA of the organism.	This occurs when peak performance has been achieved and without a change in strategy or in assumptions, the business or the technology will hit-the-wall and get into a stall.	A result of an externally initiated stimulus, generally under radar or innocuous looking, with the disruptor not even pre-gauging the extent of disruption that the change can trigger.
Needs a catalyst, energy and nutrients to support the change.	Stretched budget for research, investments planned for long-term research projects.	Budget for failure, proactive leadership.
Large-scale changes in characteristics, whether physical, emotional or intellectual.	A large scale and a large positive impact post the end-of-life event.	When fully mature, triggers an end-of-life for the current way of conducting business or application of technology; a cause of mass-extinction of competing businesses
Irreversible	Because of inherent wide acceptance by all.	Accompanied by systematic breakdown of all core assumptions; acceptance over time.
Change marked by pain but followed by sustained period of tranquility and stability.	Low or nil negative impact.	Where the market or the technology needs time to recalibrate to the new and disruptive methods. Any adoption is out of the fear of being outmaneuvered or to dip-your-toes to be at least in the periphery of the game.

delivery structures – this, in turn, also gives birth to disruptive strategies like in the case of Netflix.

8.5 In Summary

- Transformations refer to an irreversible change into something new. It could be changes in the physical, intelligence or emotional character of an entity with very little retained from the past.
- Transformation is end-of-life followed by innovation or creation.
- Transformations are of two types:
  - Generative transformations are like divergent genetic engineering
  - Disruptive transformations are akin to natures mass-extinction.
- A quick summary of transformations and their characteristics are given in Table 8.4.

Selected Bibliography – Section III

2015 International Technology Roadmap for Semiconductors (ITRS). June 5, 2015, Semiconductor Industry Association. www.semiconductors.org/resources/2015-international-technology-roadmap-for-semiconductors-itrs/

Anderson, Richard H. December 2014, Delta's CEO on using innovative thinking to revive a bankrupt airline, *Harvard Business Review*.

Brailsford, Sir Dave. March 11, 2015, Core principle and marginal gains. Video clip. www.youtube.com/watch?v=THNBIQenywc

Burridge, Nicky. May 10, 2017, Artificial intelligence gets a seat in the boardroom, Nikkei, Asian Review https://asia.nikkei.com/Business/Companies/Artificial-intelligence-gets-a-seat-in-the-boardroom

Cabibihan, John-John, Javed, Hifza, Ang Jr, Marcelo and Aljunied, Sharifah Mariam. 2013, Why robots? A survey on the roles and benefits of social robots for the therapy of children with autism, *International Journal of Social Robotics*.

Christensen, Clayton M., Raynor, Michael E., and McDonald, Rory. December 2015, What is disruptive innovation? *Harvard Business Review*.

Chu, Jennifer – Reporter. April, 8 2018, Brewing up Earth's earliest life, MIT News Office. http://news.mit.edu/2018/earths-first-biological-molecules-0409

Downes, Larry and Paul Nunes, January–February 2018, Finding your company's second act – how to survive the success of a big-bang disruption, *Harvard Business Review*.

Grover, Lov K. July–August 1999, Quantum computing, *The Sciences*.

Keane, John. February 2009, Monitory democracy, Talk delivered at the Universitat Jaume I, Castelló de la Plana, Spain.www.johnkeane.net/monitory-democracy/ or at https://youtu.be/viiFxalD3FY

Kim, W. Chan and Mauborgne, Renée. 2015, *The Blue Ocean Strategy*, Harvard Business Review Press.

Lawrence, Linda. November 1983, Thank you Delta Airlines, *Readers Digest*.

Mayerowitz, Scott. February 3, 2016 Delta Airlines CEO will retire after leading turnaround, Associated Press. https://skift.com/2016/02/03/delta-air-lines-ceo-anderson-who-led-turnaround-announces-retirement/

Nielsen, Michael. August 2008, Quantum computing for everyone. http://michaelnielsen.org/blog/quantum-computing-for-everyone/

Pascale, Richard, Gioja, Linda and Milleman, Mark. 2001, *Surfing the Edge of Chaos: The Laws of Nature and the New Laws of Business*, Crown Publishing Group.

Ponsford, Matthew and Glass, Nick. February 14, 2014, The night I invented 3D printing, CNN. https://edition.cnn.com/2014/02/13/tech/innovation/the-night-i-invented-3d-printing-chuck-hall/

Reuters and Prigg, Mark. February 18, 2015, US Government Roadmap Epigenomics Program, Recipe for the human body revealed: Ground-breaking map of human epigenomes could lead to personalised medicine, Dailymail.com www.dailymail.co.uk/sciencetech/article-2958445/Scientists-unveil-map-epigenome-second-genetic-code.html

Slater, Matt. August 8, 2012, How cycling went from tragic to magic, BBC Sport. http://news.bbc.co.uk/sport2/hi/olympics/cycling/7534073.stm

Slater, Matt. August 8, 2012, Olympics cycling: Marginal gains underpin Team GB dominance, BBC Sport. www.bbc.com/sport/olympics/19174302

Staropoli, Nicholas. July 14, 2016, Can understanding epigenetics help stave off 6th mass species extinction? Genetic Literacy Project. https://geneticliteracyproject.org/2016/07/14/can-understanding-epigenetics-help-stave-off-6th-mass-species-extinction/

Tocqueville, Alexis. April 2003, *Democracy in America: And Two Essays on America*, Penguin Classics.

University of California, Los Angeles. January 11, 2001, Liquid water at Earth's surface 4.3 billion years ago, scientists discover. *ScienceDaily*. www.sciencedaily.com/releases/2001/01/010111074038.htm

Wein, Harrison. September 27, 2010, Stress hormone causes epigenetic changes, National Institutes of Health. www.nih.gov/news-events/nih-research-matters/stress-hormone-causes-epigenetic-changes

West, Geoffrey. 2017, *The Universal Laws of Growth, Innovation and Scale – Sustainability in Organisms, Economies, Cities and Companies*, Wiedenfeld & Nicolson.

Tying It All Together

Developing Elastic Strategy Options with STA Triangles

"Straightforward actions generally lead to engagement; surprising actions generally lead to victory."

– Sun Tzu

Chapter 9

Strategy Triangles in their Entirety

Formulating Elastic Business Strategies

Failure can be continuous and repeated; so can success. There is no statistical formula that has a bias towards either of the two.

In August 1913, an extremely low-probability yet a fascinating occurrence at the Monte Carlo casino (in Monaco) wreaked havoc on the gambling world. On one specific roulette table, interest started building when the ball fell on the black several times. People started crowding around the table, betting on the red. The fallacious law of averages, they must have surmised, should have turned to red after a series of black occurrences. On the contrary, the ball kept falling on the black for a record total of 26 times before it turned to red! Gamblers lost millions and the casino made a killing that night. The gamblers had foolishly ignored that the probability of a black occurrence would always be 50% regardless of the number of times the ball had fallen continuously on a black previously.

In yet another incident years ago, the author had been assigned the task of talking some good-hearted sense to a difficult colleague. Unsuccessful and exhausted by the end of the session, the author asked him how he was planning to even modestly succeed with his attitude as he still had a significant part of his working life left. His answer saddened him. He commented, "The law of averages has to work in my favor sometime; I cannot continue to fail, as success will at some point in time catch up with me." The author did not have the heart to tell him that failures could be callously sustained and wounding unless consciously stemmed. There are no laws for self-inflicted failures. Success, on the other hand, does not come without hard work, right attitude and a bit of inspiration.

Some outcomes have a high probability of success, invariably backed by a robust execution plan, while for others, the outcomes can be completely uncontrollable. While the former can be strategized to deliver a desired outcome, the latter is purely based upon the draw of luck. Interestingly, if there were a very large number of trials for both types of occurrences, the outcomes of both would show a similar normal distribution curve. This seems to be fatalistic because whether an outcome is controllable or uncontrollable, both will always trace the omnipresent normal distribution over statistically relevant trials. One of the foremost advantages of the STA-triangles is that it can help in developing strategies that can dramatically increase the likelihood of success. In-fact, though strategy triangles are a simple representation, they have a lot of implicit boundaries and intelligence built into them, helpful in adopting an appropriate strategy in an ever-changing business environment.

9.1 STA Triangle and Selection of Strategy

When the three equidistant points on each axis are connected, three coaxial triangles are formed, as shown in the following figure (Figure 9.1). Conversely, each of the three strategy triangles is represented by three equidistant

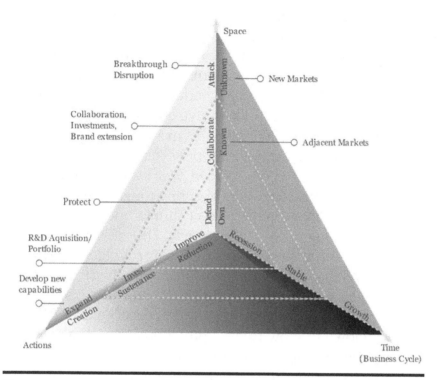

Figure 9.1   Strategy Triangles: Time–Space–Action = Strategy.

endpoints on the STA axes. The area bounded by the three lines also signifies the level of relative risk that a firm will be necessarily exposed to in following that strategy. Thus, each triangle represents the minimum business response within the boundary enclosed, below which firms are letting go of precious opportunities; this strategy has been termed by the author as the 'n' business strategy or the 'nominal' business strategy and is represented as a *time–space–action = strategy* sequence.

Among the three STA axes, the time axis always represents the true state of the market or the organization. Therefore, in selecting the relevant coaxial STA triangle, and hence the corresponding strategy, the time axis selection must correspond to the real state of the market – recession, stable or growth.

■ The innermost triangle corresponds to business responses during market recession or tight internal conditions. The firm strongly defends its 'owned' markets and spaces, and resorts to measures like internal cost reduction, improved operational efficiency and productivity improvements. It also adopts actions like active customer retention and improved satisfaction within its marketspace. However, firms should not stop just at protecting their present. They also need to *protect their future* something that most firms tend to overlook during tough times.

During recession the market shrinks and so does the spending power. Interestingly, HBR research by Ranjay Gulati, Nitin Nohria, and Franz Wohlgezogen, showed that 85% of the companies lose their momentum and struggle during the recovery period post the recession. Only 9% excelled after a slowdown to grow back to prerecession levels and the authors, through their research, understood the reasons that could help any company achieve similar results. The winners kept investing in key innovation programs and trying risky ideas even during such tight conditions.

The innermost triangle, thus, is all about protecting the core of the organization, whether its market position – current and *future*, exploiting opportunities, and retaining the customers. Consequently, it corresponds to *recession–own–reduction = protect* business strategy on the strategy triangles. The strategy not only means cost reduction but also minimum strategic investments into innovation and the future.

■ The middle triangle corresponds to business responses when the market is stable and hence the firm not only defends and invests in its own spaces but also expands through collaborations, partnerships, investments and brand extensions. The investments are deeper and wider. Firms invest in R&D, acquisitions and in known spaces to acquire new customers and launch new product offerings.

Thus, the middle triangle is the 'invest and grow' in the stable markets and corresponds to *stable–known–sustenance* = *invest* business strategy. This needs to be highly focused with a few strong winners identified and backed in the markets which are familiar and hence offer significantly higher chances of success.

One distinct strategy that the winners in this triangle adopt is Pareto's rule that states, the top 20% control 80%. Firms become bigger via consolidation, economies of scale and/or disposal of non-core assets. Large companies, like GE, keep a business only if it is within the top three in size globally. Thus, the big companies tend to become bigger.

Likewise, following the normal distribution curve assumptions rather than the power laws to drive innovation programs is also a sure road to failure. The premise is that when the whole organization is involved in generating thousands of ideas, the ubiquitous normal curve will apply, and while there will be a few ideas that are plain useless, most others will be the mediocre ones around the mean, but there must exist a few that will be stellar. But it does not! This is because innovation is a dependent variable and depends upon the organization culture, the people and their motivations, and if not aligned, it continuously flops. For innovation programs to succeed, a slight variation of the Pareto principle, the power law, also called the scaling law, needs to be adopted. David Easley and Jon Kleinberg call this the 'rich-get-richer' phenomena because of the exponential growth that it triggers after a tipping point. The power law is applicable to such increases in 'popularity' and the 'network effect.' The power law states that for a variable x, the function follows the curve $f(x) = ax^c$, where a and c are constants. Hence if x increases linearly, f(x) increases with an exponential power of x. This is also applicable to proliferation of telephones and fax-machines or ecommerce platforms, something that we discussed amply in the time–action dimension (Section 3.3).

Peter Thiel, a serial entrepreneur, uses the power law for picking every investment within his portfolio such that each must have the potential to return the entire value of the PE fund. This is a similar approach that was recommended earlier for innovation – it can only be planned based on power law and not the normal distribution law, which signifies the process of curating great ideas and an equally great execution.

Pareto's principle is extremely useful in replicating successful start-up ideas too. Though Amazon is a global ecommerce firm, countries with a vibrant start-up ecosystem do boast of players influenced by Amazon – India has Flipkart (now Walmart) and China, Alibaba. Similarly, Uber created similar copybooks and so did Airbnb. It is also interesting to note that Facebook does not have a copybook (except for in China but for a different reason). This is because in each of the former cases localization was necessary – shipments, products, taxis, hotels and home stays. Each of this required local intelligence to enlist and because the local ecommerce companies reached them faster, they grew more rapidly. In the case of Facebook, no localization was necessary and hence there weren't many copybooks. For Amazon, Uber and Airbnb, expanding to known spaces was only a matter of time and they pose an extremely stiff competition to the local players today. A corollary to Pareto is, if a segment is over-crowded it is best to leave it aside. So, a new Amazon copybook in India will need a lot of effort, differentiation and deep pockets to be widely successful.

■ The outermost triangle corresponds to a high-growth market or a high-risk/high-gain engagement, something that either does not occur often, or is not tried often. This corresponds to firms not only playing in the areas of strength and interest, but also in areas that are unrelated or distantly related – truly unknown or semi-known spaces where resources that are potentially in excess are deployed. When the time axis corresponds to high growth, both money supply as well as the consumer spending power is very high. This is where firms use the attack and disrupt strategy and hence, the outermost triangle corresponds to *growth–unknown–create = breakout/disrupt* business strategy. This region enables the firms to not only grow exponentially but warrants new capabilities that they may not have developed before. The market is buoyant and such an aggressive strategy can be easily tested.

The innermost triangle was all about being in the right side of the normal distribution curve, the middle triangle was about being in the top 20% by using Pareto's principle and the power law, but the outermost triangle is even more restricted. It is the cruelest region of the operating area. The triangle is not about success but about *failure*. Thus, the normal distribution curve, while fully applicable, represents *failure* and *not* success in this triangle. This is because while success could have partial outcomes, failure is only binary. It thus is a mirror image of the normal distribution curve of the innermost triangle – the right hand 10% represents extreme failure, the middle 80% depicts varying degree of failures and only the leftmost 10% portrays a hard struggle but a substantial degree of success. Most start-up failure reports suggest that more than 90% of start-ups fail and less than 10% survive. The extremely small percentage at the leftmost corner of the curve represents resounding success, something that the likes of Amazon, Uber and Airbnb have achieved – at the time they started, and until they had captured the market in their operating geography. Once they had established themselves their operative strategy moved to the middle triangle by expanding rapidly to 100+ countries.

The operating strategy in this triangle is predicated on disruption and we have discussed many examples in the text. Breaking down all assumptions in a conventional business and changing implicit rules behind them (e.g., power should be delivered free by harnessing energy from nature) is one such approach that defies conventional thinking. Attitudinal economics and disruptive transformations are yet others. Monetizing time value (e.g., old cloth mills in Mumbai had large tracts of lands, which grew exponentially in value over a period of 100 years) is yet another. Today monetizing insights from large accumulated masses of big data built over time will yield similar value.

The three triangles and the corresponding strategies represent a sliding scale for companies to adopt. While the inner triangle is the most conservative and a minimum must during recession, the outermost triangle signifies a high-risk, high-gain opportunity that needs to be harnessed during high-growth markets. As one moves from the inner triangle to the outer triangle for decision-making, the quantum of risk and the degree of uncertainty increases significantly. The actions for the inner triangle can be predictably prescriptive based on research and pattern; however, the actions and strategies for the outermost triangle need to take cognizance of lack of information, pattern or research, and extreme volatility in the creation of the unique, and hence, needs the preparedness to pivot and change. But the strategy and the pivot need not be based only on 'spray and pray' – the odds in favor of success can be greatly improved if the short-term strategies needed in achieving numerous short-term objectives in a dynamic environment can be maintained. It is important to note that money can be made within any triangle, but it is the entry strategy and the direction of attack that differentiates the three. It is also noteworthy that the outermost triangle is the fastest route to extremely rapid firm valuations while the inner triangle is more around managing the profit and loss and hence the route to profits but not necessarily to steep valuation multipliers.

9.2 STA Triangle and Elastic Coefficient of Organizational Strategy

From the nominal or the 'n' strategy triangle diagram, many larger or smaller triangles can be drawn representing a choice of strategy from multiple options. Whereas the time axis represents the exact state of the market or the organization, the other two axes – space and action, represent choice. Since there are three states on each of these axes, when taken three-at-a-time by selecting one from each axis, gives rise to 27 different combinations. As determined earlier and based on published research as well as wide experience of the author, firms must operate beyond the strict precincts of the 'n' strategy triangles (i.e., adopt more aggressive, flexible and *elastic* strategies with the changing business environment).

Elasticity between two dependent variables in a two-dimensional frame is defined as the degree of change caused in one due to the change in the other. However, the STA triangle is a three-dimensional representation with each of the three 'n' strategy triangles – the inner, middle and the outer triangles, representing three operational areas with vastly varying degrees of risks and outcomes. There are two kinds of *elastic* changes possible in each of these three 'n' strategy triangles – change in one vertex of the triangle on one changeable axis (space or action) (e.g., from *own* to *known*), or, change in two vertices of the triangle on both changeable axes (space and action) (e.g., from *own* to *unknown* and *simplify* to *sustain* simultaneously) – with a small reminder that the time axis continues to represent reality and hence fixed. Please note that moving from one triangle vertex to another on any axis is always a step, non-linear, change. Hence it is a discrete change and not a continuous change with significant differences in approach and assumptions. When we say 'elastic' in relation to the STA triangles, we mean 'step-elastic' – the reason why the *elastic coefficient of strategy* in the STA triangle can also be known as *coefficient of extension* of the 'n' *strategy*.

On the strategy triangles, larger triangles can be drawn from the innermost (recession) strategy triangle, referred to as n+1 or n+2 strategies. Similarly, smaller triangles can be drawn from the outermost (high-growth) strategy triangle, referred to as n-1 or n-2 strategies. The +1(+) and +2(++) or –1(–) and –2(– –) being the 'Step elastic coefficient of the organizational strategy'; the positive coefficient depicts aggressive and risk calibrated strategy while the negative coefficient depicts an inverse, conservative and risk-averse strategy. The *elastic coefficient of strategy* is defined as the *distance from the minimum core strategy on the action or space axes, the core being the 'n' strategy*.

Understanding elastic coefficient of strategy is important as it depicts diversity in approach of multiple leaders. Given the same situation, two leaders may choose two different strategies depending upon their risk-taking capacity and differential information that they may have. The triangles easily allow multitude of such strategies with their associated risk quotients that a leader can weigh in before closing on the final strategy.

9.3 Understanding the Nomenclature of STA Triangles and Elastic Coefficient of Strategy

The following steps can be used to construct the nomenclature for the *time–space–action* = *strategy* sequence.

1. Start with time: Select from Recession, Stable or Growth states.
2. Concatenate space: There are three choices here – own, known and unknown. Pairing time–space that drives high-probability successful outcomes gives recession–own, stable–known and growth–unknown.
3. Concatenate action: The three choices available are – protect, invest and breakthrough/disrupt. Pairing action with time–space combinations from the previous step with likely–probability of successful outcomes generates recession–own–protect, stable–known–invest and growth–unknown–breakthrough/disrupt, the thesis of this book.
4. These are the starting positions for a firm predicated on the current state of time axis. Hence, they are called 'n' or nominal strategies corresponding to inner, middle and outer triangles.
5. Micro and macro conditions change continuously, which changes the forecast narrative. This allows firms to either contain or increase calculated risks to move beyond the n strategy. When they adopt more

conservative strategies, they move inwards from the 'n' triangle by selecting different space and action states – this is possible while only on the middle and outer triangles. Likewise, when they adopt more aggressive strategies, they move outwards from the 'n' triangle and select different space and action states – this is possible while only on the middle and inner triangles.

6. These 27 different combinations correspond to 27 different strategies that firms can evaluate and adopt based on the time–state, whether in recession, stable or growth states.

9.4 Developing Elastic Strategies for Time in Recession – Strategies for the Inner Triangle

In evolutionary terms, recession is like a drastic business climatic change – like the ones triggered in 1980–1982, 1990–1991, 2000–2002 and then in 2008; any inability of a firm to respond to these sharp changes will likely precipitate its extinction – either in the near term or in the long term. Sustained recession or depression is a precipitator of a mass-extinction event, something that occurred in 1929 in the US.

In times of recession or during loss-making operations, protecting the core is the lowest minimum strategy. This corresponds to *recession–own–reduction* = *protect*, also termed as the 'n' or nominal strategy during recession. However, this is not enough. History is replete with instances where corporations have affected deep cost cuts as a singular strategy but failed to recover post the recession. One such example is Sony, which followed this strategy during the 2007 recession and is still struggling to recover because it ceded its position to Amazon, Microsoft and Samsung during the recession. Another stark example is Lucent, which truly stayed within the

Table 9.1 Elastic Strategies for the Inner Triangle

Core Strategy	Strategy	Time	Space	Action	Deviation from Core	Elastic Coefficient of Strategy	Curve
Protect the core (improvement & Simplification led)	Protect	n	n	n	recession-own-reduction=protect	n	Normal Distribution
	+Invest	n	n	n+1	recession-own-sustenance=protect+invest	n+1	
	+Alliance	n	n+1	n	recession-known-reduction=protect+alliance		
	+Alliance+Invest	n	n+1	n+1	recession-known-sustenance=protect+alliance +invest	Double n+1	
	++Attack/annex	n	n+2	n	recession-unknown-reduction=protect++attack	n+2	
	++Disrupt	n	n	n+2	recession-own-creation=protect++disrupt	n+2	
	+Alliance++disrupt	n	n+1	n+2	recession-known-creation=protect+alliance++disrupt		
	++Attack/annex+Invest	n	n+2	n+1	recession-unknown-sustenance=protect++attack+invest	Double n+2	
	++attack+disrupt	n	n+2	n+2	recession-unknown-creation=protect++attack+disrupt		

Action: Reduction, Sustenance, Create
Space: Unknown, Known, Own
Time Axis: Recession
Risk Quantum: Increasing Elastic Coeff of Strategy ->

inner triangle and, in fact, even over-simplified their business by separating future technology businesses rather than their current technology businesses – double impact of 'time think' and recession – to see themselves completely obliterated in a short while. Table 9.1 lists potential elastic strategies for the inner triangle.

9.4.1 The n+1 elastic, Aggressive strategies

As observed earlier, firms should operate beyond the confines of the innermost triangle during a recession. In fact, Gulati et al.'s research suggests that firms that went beyond, even in the toughest times, were far more successful than those who didn't. This has been termed as the n+1 approach on the triangles, which translates into a well-balanced and a well-diversified risk and resourcing strategy. Thus, despite the lowest minimum approach during these times being *recession–own–reduction = protect*, studies have shown that it is not enough for the long-term sustenance of the business. *Recession–own–sustenance = protect +invest* (Figure 9.2) gives a much better chance of success after the recession. The second most successful combination is *recession–known–reduction*

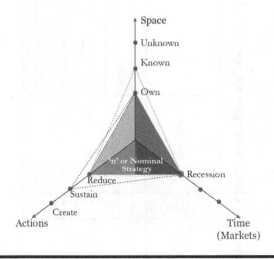

Figure 9.2   Inner Triangle: Recession – the n+1 Elastic Strategy

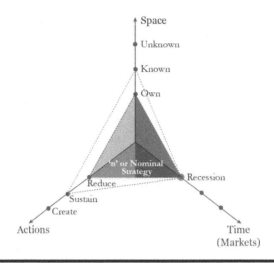

Figure 9.3   Inner Triangle: Recession – the Double n+1 Elastic Strategy

= *protect +alliance* as suggested by the same research. Both correspond to the n+1 approach as the choice of strategy is an aggressive +1 over the core strategy on one of the two other axes – space or action. A more extreme combination is possible when the +1 strategy is deployed on both the space and action axes or the double n+1 strategy (Figure 9.3). This corresponds to the *recession–known–sustenance* = *protect +alliance +invest* strategy selection.

There are many inspiring examples, and these include Amazon, Dominos and Netflix, all of whom not only survived the 2007 recession but have continued to dominate the market even 12 years after the occurrence.

9.4.2 The n+2 Elastic, Over-aggressive Strategies

There also exists the potentially over-aggressive n+2 approach (Figure 9.4). Should firms consider these aggressive outer triangle formations *recession–own–creation* = *protect ++disrupt*, or *recession–unknown–reduction* = *protect ++attack* at all? The answer to this question is a very cautionary and carefully weighted 'yes' for both the strategies.

Figure 9.4   Inner Triangle: Recession – the n+2 Elastic Strategy

Let us first try and understand what is the difference between the two strategies? 'Disrupt' is an action strategy and even a small contender can disrupt the market. On the other hand, 'attack' is a space strategy and assumes scale and resources at one's disposal. When Model X was launched, Musk was deploying the ++disrupt strategy; he knew that electric cars had a range problem and he needed better batteries for the Model X to deliver the 300 miles plus range on a single charge. Just 2400 of the Tesla Model X cars were sold but this clearly disrupted the electric vehicle market by breaking down the then existing constraints. When Musk launched the Model 3 and asked consumers to book the car with a USD 1000 deposit, he got 200,000 orders within 48 hours. This was a ++attack strategy. Tesla was not geared well for the massive scale of the attack strategy they had embarked upon and lost the sheen of their painfully established ++disrupt strategy. The recently launched Tesla Cybertruck is a different beast but was unveiled with a similar strategy. With highly divided opinion across the market, only time will tell if the strategy will continue to be ++disrupt or Tesla will attempt a ++attack once again.

9.4.3 The Double n+2 Elastic or the Hyper-aggressive Strategies

Finally, do we even consider the hyper-aggressive *recession–known–creation* = *protect +alliance ++disrupt*, OR *recession–unknown–sustenance* = *protect ++attack +invest* OR the extreme *recession–unknown–creation* = *protect ++attack ++disrupt* combinations? A resounding no as that would be opening too many fronts with both the risk and resource allocation being highly skewed and over-aggressive for the recessionary state that the market is in. In fact, the options are contradictory and make little sense. Especially for the larger firms, it is better to choose n+1 on the axes in the positive end and no more.

An oft quoted example is that of Hewlett Packard, which adopted a heady mix of all the above three strategies during the 2000 recession – they led an acquisition (Compaq), they increased their R&D spend massively, they embarked on a global rebranding exercise and also spent large sums of money to invest to increase their footprint in developing

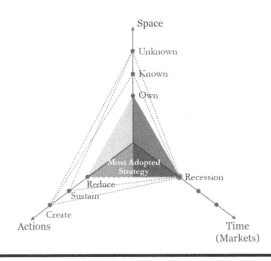

Figure 9.5   Inner Triangle: Recession – the Double n+2 Elastic Strategy

countries. Of course, their strategy failed and since then, they have tracked very poorly vis-à-vis their competitors.

9.5 Developing Elastic Strategies for Time in Stable State – Strategies for the Middle Triangle

The middle triangle is all about ecosystem expansion with both linear but mostly non-linear amplification. This is also the region where firms spend the bulk of their lifecycle maintaining and expanding their position, albeit across multiple time-periods. In evolutionary terms this is the phase of continuous mutation or variability for continuous adaptation to the changing environment. Since the operating strategy position of the firm is *stable–known–sustenance* = *invest* (or the stable 'n' strategy), companies that do not invest into the future over time wither away. In fact, the classic symptom of this triangle is that the 'big becomes bigger and the small becomes smaller.' Firms acquire similar businesses across geographies like Uber's acquisitions of similar companies in China, Russia and the Middle East, or Google creating the cloud in 2002. Operating within this triangle has the maximum flexibility because the elastic co-efficient of strategy can be safely orchestrated between +1 and –1, something that studies have shown to be most optimum for long-term growth. Adopting a more conservative, –1 elastic strategy allows the firm to pursue continuous improvement (and clean up) and is a sound strategy to follow for the business-as-usual elements; pursuing the aggressive, +1 elastic strategy, using innovation and disruption for creating products of the future is an equally important need (Table 9.2).

Table 9.2 Elastic Strategies for the Middle Triangle

Core Strategy	Strategy	Time	Space	Action	Deviation from Core	Elastic Coefficient of Strategy	Power Distribution Curve
Invest in growth (Investment Led)	-protect+reduce	n	n-1	n-1	stable-own-reduction=invest-protect-reduce	Double n-1	
	-protect	n	n-1	n	stable-own-sustenance=invest-protect	n-1	
	-reduce	n	n	n-1	stable-known-reduction=invest-reduce	n-1	
	Invest	n	n	n	stable-known-sustenance=invest	n	
	-protect+disrupt	n	n-1	n+1	stable-own-creation=invest-protect+disrupt	n+-1	
	+attack/annex-reduce	n	n+1	n-1	stable-unknown-reduction=invest+attack-reduce	n+-1	
	+attack/annex	n	n+1	n	stable-unknown-sustenance=invest+attack	n+1	
	+disrupt	n	n	n+1	stable-known-creation=invest+disrupt	n+1	
	+attack+disrupt	n	n+1	n+1	stable-unknown-creation=invest+attack+disrupt	Double n+1	

Risk Quantum: Increasing Elastic Coeff of Strategy ->

Time Axis: Stable

Space: Own, Known, Unknown — Action: Create, Sustenan, Reduct

9.5.1 The n+1 Elastic, Balanced– Aggressive Strategies

The n+1 strategies can be effectively adopted when the markets are in a steady state and the organizational performance is at par or above the market. It is a reasonable time to balance between sustaining and growth. Hence *stable–unknown– sustenance* = *invest* +*attack* as well as *stable–known–creation* = *invest* +*disrupt* are two n+1 strategies that can be adopted. Since the former is a space attack strategy (i.e., removing entrenched competition or going frontal in the competitors lair), it has higher risks, needs higher resources and is likely to generate higher returns. Take, for example, Ola, Oyo or Flipkart – the three ecommerce unicorns in India. They took head on Uber, Airbnb and Amazon, respectively, in India and posed a formidable competition.

The stable–known–creation = *invest* +*disrupt* strategy uses disruption at its core and hence has the element of stealth in it. As discussed earlier it uses the 'too-little-too-late' strategy to trounce their goliath-like competition. Earlier in the text we have also seen how Amazon destroyed brick-and-mortar bookstores or how Airbnb built a valuation that is larger than brick-and-mortar Marriott hotels.

The more aggressive 'double n+1' elastic coefficient of strategy for the middle triangle is *stable–unknown–creation* = *invest* +*attack* +*disrupt*. This has the most aggressive combination of attack and disrupt. Jio telecom deployed both of this. Reminding again, 'disrupt' is an action strategy and even a small contender can disrupt the market while 'attack' is a space strategy and needs scale and resources at one's disposal. Jio attacked a space, telecom, that was bleeding and overcrowded, using the might of its resources and disrupted the market by creating extremely unique product bundles at an unbeatable price that included free talk time for life. Musk has adopted the same mode with his three core ventures, although the technology speaks but the money is not yet ringing.

9.5.2 The n-1 Elastic or the Conservative Strategies

The n-1 strategies can be effectively adopted when the markets are in steady state and the organizational performance is at par with the market but year-on-year growth is losing momentum. The *stable–known–reduction = invest –reduce* is a strategy usually adopted when a firm is in a piquant position of having high market share but on a product that is soon getting outdated. The new version of the product needs to be built and released but only for upgrading the current customers. If the firm does not invest in creating the new product it is a matter of time before it will lose its market share to new entrants. Since the business plan can never be justified, firms will have to adopt the strategy to expand from their current markets so that the cost of building the upgraded product can be recovered largely from a new but a known market and new customers, while they can control or reduce the cost of upgrades for their existing customers.

The *stable–own–sustenance = invest –protect* strategy is adopted when current products of a firm has been rapidly outdated by evolving new technologies. For example, both the cloud and responsive UI caused a similar effect. Firms went on to do the minimum with their product upgrades (e.g., products were moved to the cloud but they were non-multi-tenanted and thus did not take advantage of the cloud infrastructure). Thus each customer had a full instance on the cloud, equivalent to the entire on-premise footprint, thereby increasing the costs of cloud infrastructure for the customer instead of a design that uses a common executable code base for all the customers but separate data instances for each. This is a mechanism firms use to protect their market share as well as their capability of acquiring new customers without disclosing a software product that is bandaged and anachronous.

Stable–own–reduction = invest –protect –reduce is a double conservative strategy that is adopted when current products of a firm are both outdated and in the end-of-life phase. Usually the incorrigible laggards are consumers of such products and the products are providing a specific lights-on function. Firms ship the minimum statutory compliance upgrade features to protect their customer base and keep the cost of maintenance as low as possible.

9.5.3 The n+–1 Elastic Strategies – The Half Conservative and Half Aggressive Strategies

These are a set of strategies that are conservative on one axis and aggressive on another. This does not necessarily denote a balance but more an execution of a plan. The *stable–unknown–reduction = invest +attack –reduce* is a strategy that has been avidly adopted by General Electric (GE). GE has a stated objective of running businesses which are either number 1 or 2 or 3 globally in terms of revenue size. It actively disposes businesses that fall below the threshold and acquires and consolidates others that it considers core. This 'attack and reduce' is a continuous 'weed and replace' strategy.

Private equities regularly use *stable–own–creation = invest –protect +disrupt*. Their primary aim is to protect their equity on one side but invest in start-ups and firms, each of which have the capability of delivering disruptive products, platforms and technologies that equals the size of the fund. Another example of deploying this strategy of 'protect and disrupt' was by Deep Knowledge Ventures, which inducted a robot as a board member with voting rights – VITAL, which we covered in disruptive transformations. Recall, DMV went on record to say that the reason why they are yet in existence in a high mortality environment is due to VITAL.

9.6 Developing Elastic Strategies for Time in Growth State – Strategies for the Outer Triangle

Though the outermost triangle is the cruelest region as 90% of enterprises venturing in this region fail, it is also the region of hope, discovery, innovation and curiosity.

In the outermost triangle, the nominal or the growth 'n' elastic strategy is all about breakout, disruption, aggression, attack, annexation and conquest – of competition, an elusive solution, an antidote to a dreaded disease or a change in attitude. Few firms can follow this strategy though because the nominal elastic strategy represents the most aggressive strategy across the entire spectrum of the three triangles and across the 27 potential strategies available to a firm. Firms adopt conservative strategies to control both their risk capital and outcomes (Table 9.3). In evolutionary terms, the outermost triangle corresponds to species innovation – just like nature adds a very few distinctive species to its repertoire over a large period not many firms with outer triangle characteristics come out successful. In fact, the failure rate is so high that only a miniscule survive.

The outermost triangle is all about creating and/or riding on the wave of boom whilst choosing a space or segment and breaking down all its implicit assumptions to unleash disruption. It could also mean unearthing and monetizing a rare or a hidden opportunity or even joining hands to achieve something humongous, like the human genome research. It could very well be about unlocking time value and the compounding effect of holding an asset like land or big masses of data.

Every page of this book is relevant to the outermost triangle simply because every strategy in this book could be used in search of the elusive success. However, three core rules are most critical

Table 9.3 Elastic Strategies for the Outermost Triangle

Core Strategy	Strategy	Time	Space	Action	Deviation from Core	Elastic Coefficient of Strategy	Curve
Attack & Disrupt (Innovation, Breakout)	-protect--reduce	n	n-2	n-2	growth-own-reduction=breakout/disrupt--protect--reduce	Double n-2	Mirrored Normal Distribution
	--protect-invest	n	n-2	n-1	growth-own-sustenance=breakout/disrupt--protect-invest	n-2-1	
	-alliance--reduce	n	n-1	n-2	growth-known-reduction=breakout/disrupt-alliance--reduce		
Growth or Disruption (Led)	--protect	n	n-2	n	growth-own-creation=breakout/disrupt--protect	n-2	
	--reduce	n	n	n-2	growth-unknown-reduction=breakout/disrupt--reduce		
	-alliance-invest	n	n-1	n-1	growth-known-sustenance=breakout/disrupt-alliance-invest	Double n-1	
	-alliance	n	n-1	n	growth-known-creation=breakout/disrupt-alliance	n-1	
	-invest	n	n	n-1	growth-unknown-sustenance=breakout/disrupt-invest		
	breakout/disrupt	n	n	n	growth-unknown-creation=breakout/disrupt	n	

Time Axis: Growth

Action: Reduct, Sustenan, Create
Space: Unknow, Known, Own

Risk Quantum: Increasing Elastic Coeff of Strategy ->

- History and previous patterns may not necessarily be of significant use.
- The decision-making is analogous to the *volatile–unknown* environment with the 'objective of the campaign' at the core with decentralized decision-making but predicated on actual 'on-the-ground' conditions.
- Adopting short phase gates and course correction strategy when entry-exit criteria has been achieved (i.e., take a series of small steps sometimes with even parallel alternatives). Follow the trail of intermediate success or achieving 'transient organizational advantage.'

9.6.1 The n Elastic Limit Outer Triangle Strategy – The Utmost Aggressive Strategy

In 2003–2004, two businesses, Alipay in China and Monitise in the UK, began operations in the same space – mobile-wallet banking. As of going to press, Alipay is an enterprise valued at USD 75 billion while Monitise from being the fastest growing company between 2012 and 2015, became a penny stock and sank from a valuation of a billion US dollars to finally being sold for a mere USD 75 million. Despite being in the very same space and creating similar technology, they veered off on separate trajectories 180° apart. The *growth–unknown–creation = breakout/disrupt* strategy is beyond just the technology. It is about how rapidly one adapts to changing needs or the opportunities being presented, and how many people were positively impacted. When Alipay was created in China, online transactions were deemed risky and not many people had the plastic power – the banks considered most of the populace as risky for giving credit. Alipay started off being an escrow for holding money paid by the online buyers and once the seller had shipped the products, the money was released. Soon Alipay saw large deposits in its accounts and from being an escrow holder became the largest mobile-wallet platform with about 500 million subscribers today. Monitise, on the other hand, chose to be a product company serving the interests of banks and credit card companies. While the latter is in no way wrong (in fact, it is a sound organizational strategy), but potentially being a b2b strategy, it had a limited impact on the people on the street. Thus, in hindsight, Monitise could not realize its strengths and the opportunities to its fullest.

Alipay has now had payment history for nearly half of the country's citizens for over one and a half decades. It generates credit scores based on past transactions. While banks in general spend USD 10–50 in running a credit check, according to industry anecdotes, Alipay does it at a few cents. Furthermore, it provides this service to the Chinese banks nearly free, thereby joining hands in improving the overall economy of the country – yet another outstanding example of collaborative attitudinal economics at play.

Further west, in India, PayTM and GooglePay have created a similar momentum. They too have close to 500 million subscribers. Today coconut sellers on sea-beaches and tea sellers on the highways, accept wallets, thus liberating a large percentage of poor in accessing the low-cost digital payment mode. There is no reason why PayTM should not be a unicorn enterprise.

Other examples also exist for *growth–unknown–creation = breakout/disrupt* (e.g., Uber, Airbnb, Facebook, Lyft – large list of start-up unicorns). However, the example of the mobile-wallet is unique because it has created the maximum impact in liberating a large proportion of have-not denizens of the east. Despite having Monitise take a lead in solving a potential problem, it viewed its strategy as *growth–known–creation* by focusing on the banks itself and hence limited its scope. Alipay and PayTM, on the other hand, slotted it differently and reaped exponential benefits.

9.6.2 The n–1 Elastic Strategy – The Slightly Conservative, Aggression in Strategy

Growth–unknown–sustenance = breakout/disrupt –invest is a conservative strategy but is the second most aggressive strategy across all the triangles. This is similar to the *growth–known–sustenance = invest* strategy but with one difference. While for the latter, a big company becomes bigger by buying similar businesses in its known spaces (e.g., Uber investing in its competitors in Russia and SE Asia), when a firm utilizes cash to buy or invest in other firms that are not in its own space but in future technologies or unknown spaces (e.g., Google buying DeepMind, a UK-based Artificial General Intelligence (AGI) company), we are referring to a *growth–unknown–sustenance = breakout/disrupt –invest* strategy. AGI, as discussed earlier, denotes deep machine learning where if a machine is faced with an unfamiliar task, it mimics the cognitive abilities of the human brain to first learn and then find a solution to the task. Jio has recently bought an AI platform to extend its capabilities.

The *growth–known–creation = breakout/disrupt –alliance* is a strategy deployed when the problem at hand is very big and needs collaboration across similar firms or institutions. One stellar example is the Human Genome Project, which is one of the biggest collaborative projects in biology that ran between 1990 and 2003 led by scientists across 18 countries to work on unearthing the sequence of over 3 million base pairs that make up the human DNA. In yet another example, on April 10, 2019, 200 scientists across the globe used an array of ten radio telescopes, synchronized by technology, to mimic one large telescope capable of capturing large wavelengths; this is how the 'shadow' of the black hole located at the center of Messier 87 galaxy was captured.

A very similar strategy to that above is the *growth–known–sustenance = breakout/disrupt –alliance –invest* strategy.

While in the preceding case, collaborators came together to solve a problem and when it is resolved went back to their respective vocations, in pursuing the *growth–known–sustenance = breakout/disrupt –alliance –invest* strategy, partners engage subsequently for the sustenance lifecycle too. The open source movement is one such example.

9.6.3 The n–2 Elastic Outer Triangle Strategy – Balance between Reward, Risks and Closure

A small but excellent molecule research lab based out of New York is researching a very novel method of treating cancer. They have synthesized paramagnetic nano-magnets (paramagnets are weak magnets that achieve this property under the influence of an external magnetic field; unlike ferromagnets they lose their magnetic property once the field is removed) that can be targeted to a cancer affected organ with a sufficiently high concentration of drugs at the tumor site. This thus improves the effectiveness of the treatment and at the same time reduces the side effects of the drug due to otherwise large quantities needed for oral or injectable delivery.

This wonderful mechanism has been under the FDA review for a significant amount of time, due to obvious reasons – it needs to be safe for human consumption. However, the lab is small and continuously in need of funds to keep the research momentum. However, they do not want external funding at this stage because of the obvious dilution impact; lack of funds, on the other hand, have slowed down the process. The *growth–unknown—reduction = breakout/disrupt –reduce* is a Hobson's choice firms have to contend with when they are faced with a shortage of funds at an extremely critical juncture. Most non-well-funded start-ups or labs running long gestation projects are often faced with such a situation. This is also the cause for large shutdowns. Firms resort to such premature abandoning of the core too fast while there are common-sensical ways of avoiding it, including allowing early investors to make money.

The *growth–own–creation = breakout/disrupt –protect* is yet another mechanism for the PE funds to invest in start-ups and growth firms. The money supply is high but according to Peter Thiel, the author of *Zero to One*, funds need to invest into every idea or firm that is capable of returning the entire value of the fund – also called the power law. Only then can the funds survive – or at least it gives a fighting chance for discovering a few unicorns.

The *growth–known–reduction = breakout/disrupt –alliance –reduce* is one answer to the quandary that start-ups or companies with low cash find themselves in, while pursuing *growth–known–reduction = breakout/disrupt –reduce* strategies. Usually leverage or dilution of equity to PEs is adopted, of course, based on the firm's operating practices to fuel the experiment on disruption. Living on shoestring budgets till that point in time is the 'reduce' strategy that such firms assiduously follow.

Just before Uber went for its IPO, the prospectus that it released showed a stark strategy followed by *growth– own–sustenance = breakout/disrupt –protect –invest*. Uber acquired businesses like itself across geographies in China, Russia and the Middle East, and despite losses in its current operations has made USD 12.5 billion on paper by exiting from its investments in some of the geographies. At the same time Uber continues to invest money in autonomous taxis as well as air-taxi services as the products of the future – on its continuous innovation journey of breakout and disruption.

Growth-own-reduction = breakout/disrupt –protect –reduce is the most critical strategy that start-ups and firms facing volatile environments adopt. They use short stage gates to deliver innovation quickly, coupled with pivot or change as a strategy to simultaneously protect themselves from impending failure and closures by also reducing the burn. This is a triple-pronged strategy that is quite well balanced in these high-risk, intense environments. Thousands of start-ups have knowingly, and sometimes unknowingly, adopted this strategy.

9.7 Unified Application

A moot question is, are the 27 different combinations that correspond to 27 different strategies firms can adopt on the STA triangles, the super set of all strategies? Furthermore, are these 27 strategies enough to cover all possible business conditions? The STA triangles is a 3D model that is a combination of space–time–action, the three *fundamental variables* that control outcomes, for effective selection of a business strategy. It tries to mimic a 'business twin.' On the STA triangles each axis is a triad of three atomic states that covers the entire range of possible occurrences – from the best to the worst. Let us now select nine states instead of the three. Taking the time axis as an example, instead of the three given states (i.e., recession, stable and growth), if we had drilled further down to three additional sub-states within each state – i.e., depression, recession and economic-stagnation instead of recession alone (or expansion, growth and boom, instead of just growth) – the granularity of the scale on each of the axes would have increased by a factor of three. If a similar approach was adopted on all the three axes, instead of 27 combinations we would end up with 9×9×9 or 729 combinations. This means that the likelihood of achieving a more accurate model would have increased by 27 times! How much more valuable can this be? Probably if the dataset of companies being researched is very large (e.g., in an academic research), such an expansion of sub-states could be useful, but for most applications of strategy evaluation, the STA triangles in the current form and the author's research is quite wide ranging and powerful to be used as a baseline.

The second question is, can intelligent machines and artificial intelligence help leaders in selection between tough alternatives? The answer again is no, as the machine can take quantitative decisions quite easily and apply it with consistency; but environments are complex and the 'consciousness' in decision-making can be difficult to be built in. Given the same situation, two top-notch leaders may take two very different decisions, sometimes even against the grain of common sense, but both could be deemed successful because it is not only the core objective of the 'campaign' but multiple side objectives that are equally important. Autonomous car tests have shown that if a dummy is thrown in front of a car and the control remains with the car, the chance that the dummy survives is many times higher than if the control were passed back to the driver. So, who should get the control under such an eventuality? The answer is obvious since the objective of the campaign is to save the pedestrian. But what should the algorithm be if there was a truck hurtling behind the car and if the car slammed the brakes the occupants in the car would face a certain death? Remembering the primary objective of the campaign (in this case, of the car) is to keep the occupants safe, the autonomous car would run over the pedestrian. But is this how a human driver would react? Possibly not. In one case she may try and save the pedestrian and, in the process, get herself killed; in another, the driver may be unable to save either. But in yet another happy case she may have been able to save both the pedestrian and her own self. Hence it is not just the main objectives but the multitude of side objectives that complicates decision-making. The STA triangles give a unique ability to give a 3D view simultaneously across the three axes hence making it much more powerful than most other mechanisms.

Our opening story was about a human error precipitated due to malfunctioning sensors in an aircraft thus confusing the aircraft systems as well as the pilots. The pilots forgot to nosedive to come out of a real stall and the plane went down into the ocean. Fast forward to March 2019, a similar set of chilling conditions – a malfunctioning angle-of-attack indicator triggering a faulty stall warning *despite* the aircraft *not* being in a stall. Reports confirm that the on-board computers took control disallowing the pilots any maneuver and forced the aircraft into a series of nosedives – a correct procedure for countering a stall, but the stall never existed in the ill-fated Boeing 737-Max aircraft. The result, another disaster, only this time it was not the pilot's error but the intelligent MCAS that caused the crash.

The truth is that we will need to learn to co-team with our artificial-intelligent humanoids, co-workers and machines. The leadership of tomorrow will be different and new roles like man–machine teaming manager, machine-risk officer or algorithm bias auditor who ensures algorithms are following ethics and guidelines to avert any mishap, will be critical organizational elements of the workplace of tomorrow. Billions of sensors will invade our lives bringing unimaginable gains, but they will malfunction occasionally. The machines will need to be trained to understand their critical limits and learn when to call for human help.

Finally, can a generic business model, validated by researching and correlating across a statistically relevant sample size, ever become a scientific law? If it were possible, then the number of true data points needed would be infinite – every case tested needs to be true. The simple answer thus is that this can never be achieved. The real reason is the law of entropy.

Most swathes of the universe are cold and freezing while there are some fusion-powered cosmic entities that generate the much-needed heat. Heat energy always flows from hot to cold objects achieving the equilibrium when the temperature of the two bodies becomes the same. This process can never be reversed without expending external energy. Moreover, no conversion or transfer of heat energy can be fully efficient as some heat is always lost (e.g., due to radiative heat loss or due to friction). This unusable or wasted heat energy when heat is transferred between objects of different temperatures is called entropy. The universe is thus in a state of perpetually increasing entropy, due to the inefficient loss of heat energy that dissipates in the universe. Since heat increases the random movement of atoms and molecules, it increases disorder. Entropy thus increases disorder, and as entropy is continuously increasing, so is disorder. Entropy is nature's way of injecting variability and uncertainty. It is also the nature's method of giving the sense of time.

Firms and the markets within which they operate are thermodynamic entities. High energy and fluctuating organizational expressions, keeps the entropy levels continuously high and perpetually increasing. This increases disorder, which alters the firm's internal and external market configurations continuously. Environments change rapidly, and governments and central banks try to bring back the order. As entropy is continuously increasing, the organizations that were the heroes of the older period either transform into something new or give way to new firms. New frameworks are then developed to understand the secret of their success only to see those disintegrate within another passage of time.

Time, space and action are fundamental in managing outcomes making the STA model stable – only the actions need to be improvised and made finer in congruence with changing times. For successful outcomes, a constant scan of the changing environment is needed to respond effectively to counter ill-effects and ride on the opportunities being presented, the blueprint of which has been abundantly elaborated.

9.8 In Summary

- The interplay of areas bounded by all three axes gives potential strategy to adopt.
- When three equidistant points on each axis are connected, three coaxial triangles are formed. Each of these represents minimum strategy as well as level of relative risk. This is termed the 'n' or the nominal strategy.
  - Three strategy triangles equate to conservative, stable and aggressive strategies. This is also called as times relevant **'n' strategy**.
  - Under recessionary or loss-making conditions, protecting the core is the lowest minimum or 'nominal' strategy.
  - The stable market is about ecosystem expansion with linear and non-linear amplification,
  - The growth periods witness firms playing beyond their areas of strength in unknown or semi-known spaces often making this the cruelest region as enterprises often fail; in short, the growth region is about breakthrough, disruption, attack and annexation.
  - But staying within the precincts of the 'nominal' strategy triangles is not enough. Existing research shows that firms must move beyond the core or the minimum, measured by the elastic coefficient of strategy. The more the elastic coefficient of strategy, the greater is the risk and consequently the prize.
- Since each axis is represented by a triad of three atomic states, 27 different strategy combinations with a wide range of possible occurrences in business environment ranging from worst to best, become possible.
- The elastic coefficient of strategy of −2 to +2 becomes possible, from the most conservative to most aggressive.

- Understanding the elastic coefficient of strategy is important as it depicts diversity in the approach of multiple leaders.

Selected Bibliography – Section IV

Easley, David and Kleinberg, Jon. 2010, *Networks, Crowds, and Markets: Reasoning about a Highly Connected World*, Cambridge University Press.

Frick, Walter. May–June 2019, How to survive a recession and thrive afterward, *Harvard Business Review*.

Gulati, Ranjay, Nohria, Nitin and Wohlgezogen, Franz. March 2010, Roaring out of recession, *Harvard Business Review*.

Loomis, Carol J. August 2011, Why Carly's big bet is failing?, Fortune Classics. https://fortune.com/2011/08/21/why-carlys-big-bet-is-failing-fortune-classics-2005/

Lopez, Linette. March 2018, The robots are killing Tesla, www.businessinsider.com. www.businessinsider.com/tesla-robots-are-killing-it-2018-3?r=UK&IR=T

Martin, Roger L. January–February 2019, The high price of efficiency, *Harvard Business Review*.

Smallwood, Karl. August 2015, The man who broke the bank at Monte Carlo: Bonus facts. www.todayifoundout.com/index.php/2015/08/man-broke-bank-monte-carlo/Monte Carlo

Stafford, Tom. January 2015, Why we gamble like monkeys, www.bbc.com, BBC. www.bbc.com/future/story/20150127-why-we-gamble-like-monkeys

Thiel, Peter and Masters, Blake. June 2015, *Zero to One*, Virgin Books.

Uber's IPO filing documents, April 2019.

Index

Page numbers in *italic* denote figures and in **bold** denote tables.